JOURNEYS ACROSS BREATH

Journeys Across Breath

Poems 1975–2005

Stephen Watts

With an afterword by Gareth Evans

PROTOTYPE · 2022

Contents

VIII. *Strands, Clusters ...*

Journeys Across Breath

Stephen Watts

I.

The Lava's Curl

From The Islands

One day I went over the mountain
and the perfect curve of air broke in two
against rock all around me. And I went down
into the strained calculus of that coast
past the white-shat cliffs of nesting cormorants,
the schist crests of that stilled and dancing land
and I lay on a slab beside the tilting sea,
the mountain like a dumbed animal at my back,
a lobster boat falling and rising in one place
and a chunk of talc in my hand, its harsh
eroded alignment giving to my fingernail,
making a lighter slit into the darkening green.
And then slowly, to the slower circling of fulmars,
a stubborn music and the far-off yellow-headed diver,
the sea disappeared and the earth became quite still.
And the two became one plate and began to move
tilting easily and veering about a single point.
And the air became like a reversed gannet
rushing back towards me, solid spray of water,
disgorged fish, bandaged sun, calm woven flowers,
origin grasses, herring shoals biting dry air,
hawk and heron that are independent of us.
And the perfect curve broke in two again and from
out the separated cones rose everything I have
ever been through, flowing inside me once
                    more ...

Gramsci & Caruso

There were a few warmed tables then :
oak were some, and less mahogany
walnut, hazel, and the tulip tree
when history was brushing us against the grain.
Gershom Scholem was alive and Walter Benjamin
and Gramsci was a child and my grandfather
heard Caruso sing to soldiers near Milan
and walked the sheep down paths through Edolo
on the way from Precasaglio to Cremona.
Anna Akhmatova was alive and Osip Mandelstam
and Blok had gone to Rome and to Ravenna
and the round bays swelled with sunlit stone
to beat within our lives down all this time.
Isaac Rosenberg was alive in Stepney still
and walked with Gertler on the Mile End Waste
past Narodiczky's printshop on the right
and milk-churn alleys where the horses fed
and sweated basements windowed to the road.
The sweat machines are in the basements still
and send back money to villages in Sylhet.
Abdus Shahid's selling vegetables off a cart.
It seems they all are older than they seem
and all of our fresh memory is washed unclean.
This time from our end of the unreal years
we look back down the century's real throat –
Me and Shahid, my dead grandad and the rest –
to where all metaphor was messed with hate :
O how lovely then to be alive, how lovely ...

*

So what's next for us, Antonu Su Gobbu ?
Childhood spent between Ghilarza and the sea.
Each autumn comes round the edge of the earth
as partisans get down off mountains in the snow.
Winter arrives sheeted with hard haemorrhaging.
And snow wreiths cover folds of sunnied pasture.
This is northern and cold. Sleet under a coat
that melts on arms and groins by curls of hair.
This guard-dog city. This bleak trade in food.
Hungry workers getting home. Bad bronze smell.
Tea basins steaming in the ripe coloured nights.
Flags of ignorance swung out for the homelands.
Or a decade borne by the breath of great singing.
These are the early years of a European century,
smell of burnt oxygens, wisps of human flesh.
Just think of it ! Pancakes drenched with curds,
Thick loaves of yellow polenta and mutton gravy,
crisp stalks of broccoli and quick-scorched corn,
stands of oranges and pomegranates and olives,
tables of sunflowers and cheeses and mild oils.
This is the market, Antonu, of a southern city :
a hunger palace where dawns are always sour
and dark-tiled tenements topple over torrents.
Goats are barking on dry and tawny pastures.
This is the history of our language, Antoninu,
shared speech come to resemble a clotted sanity.
Why has language – the lucid and cogent – got
us to this deathfeast, Antonu, in our European
century far from home ... ?

*

Don't worry. Ninuzzu. Don't fret.
Sta bene. Ninno. Ninarriedu. Sta bene.
When the sun makes the tiny flowers breath,
then it's hot enough for harvest hay to sprawl
in the sweated labour of the fields and walls
in the valleys of Tonale and the Val Aperte.
Maria Buona is working her guts out still,
Bortolo's appendix has not burst in the snow.
Coming down from Pezzo, Ida and Esterina
have slid slowly off the cart of moving hay.
(Esterina's now a nun! Ida's eighty today!)
The sun sings. And your fields are still there.
In Tonale and Gavia. And the tired sun sings.
And there is work for you now in Precasaglio
about the ceilings and walls and curling hills
and your daughters will grow with the pasture
and they will not have to live in a city alone.
Sta bene, ninno. For surely this is not a dream.
The mountains are still there with their teeth
it is not they will rip you from needed work.
Trees at the meadow's edge flail in the wind
it is not they will tear our lives to these shreds.
O ninuzzu, this is not a dream – those other
things never happened : the pains in the gut,
haemorrhagings in the head congesting time,
pressure of all history forced on one moment.
Explosion of blood in the dark sky of the head.
Adders bit wild strawberries, tart their taste.
Look! The angel of history has turned round
and is looking back at us from our own future.
It is all right. Stay calm. Everything is fine.
Where the torrent plummets on steep houses
you are there, you are still there, you are
                    surely still there ...

A wooden bridge, ponted to the river.
A small hay-cart pulled by a hayless horse
through pine woods to the pass of La Rosa
or into Ponte di Legno at the end of the war ...
Pine nuts for journeyings and also for jams
and weeks at the frontier awaiting passports.
My grandfather walking to Sant Apollonia
through pine woods on his daughter's arm
to play bocce with the innkeeper, and then
up the sheepwalks toward Passo di Gavia,
or to Pezzo for sharp and tiny coffees with
his class contemporary, the Pezzo priest.
Bortolo on the snow with his appendix burst
the black words spilt into London by post.
Partisans getting down off sleety hill-stations
in the white war of the first winter ascents.
Shot close to their homes. Then the centre
of the mountain town – torn out by bombs.
History then set economic bombs all its own
to burst against your calm working later on.
Uncomely time. Blue phantom of summers.
The lack of choice in the harshness of lives,
even in Europe, even in those near years.
Bare walls. And the pocked eyes of houses.
Haycarts moving through hill towns at night.
My grandfather, a man nearing fifty, his
moustache the thickness of a fisted finger.
And blood about to explode inside his head.
A caterpillar. A butterfly. A migrant. Such
times in a life.

Hölderlin In The Auvergne

He was walking through the Puy
in the dead volcanic days of winter
and felt the heats off the cold rock.
Magmas welled up in his memory :
He saw them coiling about Europe.
"Look" he said "docile feldspars,
cryptic horneblendes, their needles,
those blue tourmalines and micas.
Look at them, the slow circuiting of
nerve ends, the choice between love
and eruption, the plaintive birdsong,
the snakes making off the hillsides.
I am all of these, the curls of lava
and the cooled aftermath together."
Soon he'll go down to the wet-fields
of the Périgord, their spring streams
diving into sleek and seagone rivers,
their fruit trees bursting to the air
and birds dipping beaks in the dew.
"Let me tell you : the things at the
remote edges, they are at the heart
of our world, they always will be,
when all else has been destroyed,
soil and archaeology of our souls."

Lord In Dream

Lord in dream I was lifted out of London
and sailed above the branny floors of
the earth. I went north over Scotland and
reached Barra and hovered over Uist like
a sick kestrel and looked down at islands
strung out like pearls about the gorge of
the western sea – good corn stooked up –
and got to Iceland in wakes of blue air.
There on the brindled moor lay a hall –
not a supermarket of packages and food
but the library of a culture not unearthed
and thought printed in its bright language.
Until a cool thermal took me and I rose
above the scattered seas and saw gross
continents off to my sides fissuring the
placid frightened ocean. And I could see
another half of me gone east past Europe
and scattered barques sitting off Mumbai.
Between Himalaya and scorched Deccan
people as sediment compressed and hurt
in the first stages of rock-making, stunned
as a mother is when her born baby's died.
But I climbed still on the thermal gyre,
could cling to the golden vessel of ropes
or toss it easy from my sky and my history.
A sick weapon that makes of us fragments
would strike me from such abrupt heights,
Lord in dream I was lifted off this earth.

The Verb "To Be"

(i.m. Arshile Gorky)

Sun, you dervish in the dancing tree
that glints and points and slowly spins
its fulcrum centred on the will to see.
You are lucid like the panels of light
and flow inside this archaic hall that
language is : you break and scatter and
in the rift, you create yourself anew.
You are the sudden sea-song of starlings
that bursts a tree at the shoreline edge.
You are blue spruce on the rim of frost.
You are a field of gauntly pecking swans
and the first November snow that tricks
the hill – cud of flower and cow's bell.
You are green, green on the inward lips
of hot night and you are the colour opal
in the human eye of the word. You are
the lucid void between blue mountains
and the eye that sees. You are the falcon
that plunges down coiling gusts of need.
You are my language, you are my speech
and you are a million years old and you
are silent, sun you circling spun dancer
in the still centre of the body's tree : sun,
you definition in the flesh of the child,
                    of the verb to be.

Marina

(i.m. Marina Tsvetaeva)

Marina if you were not dead you would
be older than these old women, scarved and
drinking in their public pride and getting
home in the cool nights where cats scurry.
In your mind words exploded – they pistoned
and shunted like dark magma and shot out
volcanic gobs and flared at the earth's edge.
And there were no gaps between your words
and their facts, the spurt and retraction of
feeling, this earth lived in and so described.
Marina – marine – sea-gone river – curtailed
ocean – heaved earth – placid inward sea –
feart wave – Marina – ocean – peace at last –
from the gashed maw of land from its mouth
coloured flecks shot cirrus into your words,
where the volcano is pierced in thin crusts
it shot glazed pelt into your air made skin.
This earth has bubbles they are your words
this earth has bubbles are unloved women
this earth has a crust pierced by hot muds.
And crazily crazily you were sucked down
to the silence of cold nights and a lost
                    grave.

Fragment ...

       ... And so I long for snow to
sweep across the low heights of London
from the lonely railyards and trackhuts
– London a lichen mapped on mild clays
and its rough circle without purpose –
because I remember the gap for clarity
that comes before snow in the north and
I remember the lucid air's changing sky
and I remember the grey-black wall with
every colour imminent in a coming white
the moon rising only to be displaced and
the measured volatile calmness of after
and I remember the blue snow hummocks
the mountains of miles off in snowlight
frozen lakes – a frozen moss to stand on
where once a swarmed drifting stopped.
And I think – we need such a change,
my city and I, that may be conjured in
us that dream birth of compassion with
reason & energy merged in slow dance.

Camões' Voyage To Goa

Ha-aa ! You made it. With one eye
and a cold in the head, leaving behind
some dangerous love, with duplicities
and arguments over precedence, some
tense anguish in a patron's convoluted
schemings. Well-timed – you got out.
From one western seaboard to another
with all the granites melting down to
human bone. Should we consume what
we seek ? Rather lie rocking, a barque
upon its tilted sea. The continuum and
its chasm. Plunging even then into an
earth that was cold and extinguished,
in that era opening onto a new world.
The roman alphabet drenched your lips
a breeze from off the sea opened pores
in your flesh, as tunny suck out hot air.
And the memory of her tawny body is
wine poured down your throat. White
teeth that could bite into your mollusc
flesh whether you hid or not. You went
ten thousand sea-miles away from home
so you could get back inside your skin.
In one moment of dream the charted air
became dance. If they thought any ship
would veer off the edges of the oceans,
you knew any body could fall deep in
past all of its selves to land on hot and
fertile coastlines glowing with dawn.

*

From one granite to another
more ancient. This rock carved to red
temple. Now dravidian script has been
written through your roman portuguese.
Aah, that was right. Gravity and grace.
Mastery of the sea and of words and of
tongues. All that is matter is deception.
The stilled dance, the stark alternatives.
Your old, blunt, sea-gonged perspective
gushes right down to our own. Did you
see the angel of history looking for us ?
Angel of maggot. Ashes and diamonds.
Ah ! Haa ! You made it. The São Bento
coming into the mouth of the red river
left you in that gilded unpassioned city
where the sea and air crashed together
in mud and liquid explosions of people.
Should we throw our art out overboard
because our barge is plunging in a tilted
sea ? All seas tilt and all our alternatives
are become few and stark and desperate.
That night you dreamed of a black hole,
as if out there the great earth was being
    sucked through its own horizon ...

*

You remember it all ! Far-off,
docile lover, merchant in word-dreams.
Otters are not languid, it is their skins

glinting the dazed cylinder of the seas,
then they slap hard water with concern.
Other ways of being your sisters knew,
honour to the goddess breathing life on
granite so it would fuse as supple bone.
Some got drowned with too much pain.
Seabirds in the burning air. So you saw
the thin wavy lines where they breathe,
the black flick of the horizon round its
copper belt. And sunlight being pelted
about tired eyes. Sand-bars and foams
that were the acts of love, their precise
bodies whirling off into rendered space.
You can remember ! Ha ! Her dream face.
And your hand on her belly that became
deep home and sanctuary for all hunger.
She is still there, thousands of sea-miles
round the stretched curves of the earth.
This place of drought and flowers. And
the sea in all its horizons pelting water,
in all its slowness, the huge gulps of it
slapping to burst your belly from within.
There are so many alternatives in a life,
the brief spasms of our calmed memory.
The body is a republic : a risk, a dream.
At one pulse, glowing air genders dance
pulling through the horizon's black hole.
Luís you saw all this, in shared Malagasi
penury and wrecked on Cambodian seas.
Your body : a new earth glitters at dawn.

*

And do you remember Coimbra.
Coimbra with its darker arches of blood
its centuries of knowing turned to stone.
Coimbra with its supermarket of suburb
and maize plots smelling faintly of salt.
With Portugal in your dreams you recall
the sea, that placid and frightened bird.
That uterus with its own milk – the sea.
Did you ever realise – dom Luís – that
slowly pulsing water was the womb out
which you would continually be reborn.
The Tagus riding you home on the night.
Or Lisbon, that shattered shore of people.
Or the Chinese, your lover, whose body
sunk in storm water at the Mekong's lip,
her salutary flesh, her endless weepings.
The women of Goa you could not stand,
their merchandise, their rich and furtive
patrons. All the people you loved and
did not love. Months stranded with debt
and lethargy in Madagascar, the death of
Diogo do Couto, the harbour bar of home.
Someone said : in our moments of despair
we talk and write to the dead – so we do.
But you in your last years of pure despair
talked only to the future, and saw us laid
out like cloths on the shattered body of
time. I can still hear your breathing ...
    Listen, Luís, now to mine.

Góngora On His Deathbed

To be alone on an island is a consolation !
But to be alone in Córdoba lasts a lifetime.
Tawny women wash in the Guad-el-Kebir
and dark riders go by in long-tailed cloaks.
What is happening in this atmosphere with
changing air ? Where am I that I am so alone
in stillborn peace ? Blood of Córdoba, town
of Moors, now the shutters are being closed.
Now Góngora's dead in a room made fragrant
with quince and orange blossom and nutmeg,
while outside luminous clouds try to disperse
and in a corner Quevedo and Ibn Arabi wait.
A little later his soul – the soul of Góngora –
well-sculpted and thus flawed to perfection –
this gold sandalled, crimson furbished soul
will leave the room through a pastel window
and climb in cloud the ladder it has thrown
back on Córdoba when it hits the solid sky.
The shape of Polyphemus extending a hand.
These things Góngora from his deathbed sees
and that three centuries later García Lorca's
body would be thrown in a ravine of stone –
Federico, a bloodied horse racing past him
on that easiest of journeys up the ladder
                    bathed in light.

Funeral Procession of Queen Eleanor

Coloured light and curtains of glass.
Beneath the vaulted ceiling – your eyes,
your swaying body that is creamy stone
and rises from fine drapery to a crown,
your face has had emery paper across it,
spat red sand streaming over your skin,
your nose and crease of mouth are gone
mouth that uttered delicate shorn song,
your king and lover in a stubborn trance
only your self to sway your body's bole,
& only you to calm the dancing branch.
Curtains of limestone, cream caen stone
and red buttresses of dry compacted sand
stand across my vision, blunt my sight.
Tell me, are you still awake ? Crosses
that once were pillars or poles, rock eggs
I've sculpted them at the meadow's edge,
endless columns for the arched blue sky.
Though we do not believe in monarchies,
though we must live in a republic of dogs.
The tired & dancing column on the road
has risen and rotated in its creamy void.
You are not dead ! O, how could you be !
Maggots of language. The body's a tree
that sways its flag across love to death.
Through the destroyed towns and fields,
plague columns of speech entering cities.
Look – they've got through – do you see :
right to the fever-house of our breathing
right to the cool vault where our lucid
                    blood resounds.

The Old Canal Barge

In another life I must have been an old-time
barge that worked the Milano-Bergamo canal,
then I would have carried all types of cargo
and people without the exacting constraints,
conscripts on their way to barracks off from
weeping mothers and newly married peasants
with their rolled mattresses for a trousseau,
herders with pig or sheep, and children back
to the magnolia interiors of their convents,
trees and wooden clogs, rope for grimaldis,
priests and soldiers and parasolled madames,
and I would have gone back and forth taking
the mountains to the sun, heaving the karst
tense of summer over winter's shattered ice.
And I might have carried my grandfather in
his soldiering days or my mother during her
youth as later she would carry the foetus me
in the salt and temerity of her body. And I
would have had no trouble with my speech,
language all the time being cured inside me
like a salami by the words of my travellers
in the cool cornered bulkheads of my cargo.
And in the 1930s – the air-deprived years –
the need for barges gone, I would have been
sunk in some backwater to rot in calm ease
with poles put through my caulking boards,
before the fascisms of the spirit could empty
villages of their homes and erupt the ritual
                    abolition of time.

Brick Lane

*(after the death of Altab Ali,
and for Bill Fishman)*

Whoever has walked slowly down Brick Lane
   in the darkening air and a stiff little
          rain,
past the curry house with lascivious frescoes,
past the casual Sylheti sweet-shops and cafés
and the Huguenot silk attics of Fournier Street,
and the mosque that before was a synagogue
         and before that a chapel,
whoever has walked down that darkening tunnel
         of rich history
from Bethnal Green to Osborne Street at Aldgate,
past the sweat-shops at night and imams with
         hennaed hair,
and recalls the beigel-sellers on the pavements,
   windows candled to Friday night,
would know this street is a seamless cloth, this
         city, these people,
and would not suffocate ever from formlessness
         or abrupted memory,
would know rich history is the present before us,
laid out like a cloth – a cloth for the wearing –
with bits of mirror and coloured stuff,
and can walk slowly down Brick Lane from end
         to seamless end,
looped in the air and the light of it, in the human
         lattice of it, the
blood and exhausted flesh of it, and the words
   grown bright with the body's belief,
and life to be fought for and never to be
         taken away.

City Of The Sun

What do you do
when you no longer have a city
you can love ?

What do you do
when you know that your language
has betrayed you ?

(for language, like
a salami, must be cured in the winter
pain of the pig of all speech)

What do you do
when you realise you have no
contemporaries in the white city
                 of the sun ?

Bloodied slaughterhouse of language.

Only when I have gathered to myself
such words in love can I say that
        I know how to speak.

Tongue, You Wild Sweetmeat

Tongue, you piece of red meat
you – liar – who tells the truth,
what words squirt off your surfeit,
all poetry fades and does not cope
or instance help or change a thing,
neither does it evade or praise,
tongue, lolling piece of red meat
slit of the face that gives no birth,
gism of words that beckon nothing
you hover-hawk of withheld speech,
you word-floater rooted in gristle,
not knowing the slow coils of pain
tongue, tongue you wild sweetmeat
curling round in your own power,
curved snake of the throat's desire
words will break you to movement,
tongue, you red animal of raw need
you – instilled with life's cravings,
half sanctioned at my skin's edge,
tongue, tongue, you always eaten
      piece of returning meat

Moors Above Walsden

The muds are dried.

Their peeling skins. The delicate
shifting patterns of their dusts.
What does my footprint matter here.

Arc of the sky and of the sun.

You can bounce slowly on the muds
without falling to the mouth below,
and feel your resonance coming back
from the rock hearth of its depths.

Dear earth. Dear erotic earth.

The pebbles are the body
sifted in the white rust of time.
The rocks that are melting at
such depths are inside me.

White words we are left with.

There must be.

Another way of being. Another
            way to be.

II.

Twenty-Four Hours

Twenty-Four Hours

(These are the hours of the day, between the earth and the air)

when the world awoke from the delirium of the aurora, blond lilies did a dance for the child and apricots grew from the sun

jams and honeys among the bindweed excited the fibula of a very large bee

a crow drank the juice of a solitary violet and flew without wings to the hillside

night bats and the demon sank in funeral jars and crystals of almandine and amethyst leapt in the womb

at nightfall your mountain became my house

the mouth of the cave was sealed with the eye of a blue horse and the men sat up hunkered by the dying embers. the women, out hunting that night, did not come back

reindeer howled in the ravines and the glaciers almost returned. the last bear descended in front of the first gyrating boulder. despots of light were ground away in the fury of nocturnal waves. crags gathered in inky moons and frozen footprints pursued the soul of man over these precipices

at first light, nightwools were carefully stripped from the child's throat, snows shuddered from the brows of the child, and drifting veils appeared before his eyes in the first fabled hour when a purple phantom rises from your cloak until the morning does not come, it is all right, i am here, i am still here. when the rivers flow with grass and the lakes with burnished gold, when there is blood in the moon and dust in the rose, when the street drops into the rut and the popular song is murmured in the calcified bone and you are led through the martial chaos and the trading of all ages, in the darkness and the thunder and the rain, it is all right, i am still here. from where the white parasols sway in the lapis lazuli and pianos play of their accord in snow caverns below icy candelabra, and skies flow down which have persisted for eternity in the breach, in those places and at the edge which cataracts into the abyss, behind waterfalls where bats gorge on blanched fingers and well nurtured eyes, or where the great plain rises once more with dust as the hunting hordes play havoc with your nerves and your soul is set on fire by the night, do not worry, i will be there, i will still be there. death and the rider might set off in pursuit of some polar hurricane or some polar vitriol or the wild antelope that grazed the soapstones of the interior, or mongol hordes flow towards the last mountain sanctuaries of tibet and turkestan, burning all the crops and farmholdings in their frenzy. but do not worry, i will be there, i will still be there.

*

in this house here the linden trees have bonnets like old dutch grandmothers and slowly nod their ribbons to and fro. the wooden benches heave among the grass that lacks chains, the buttercups, the iron palisades, and the dead voices of children roll in trance over the hyacinthine river. the man is gentle and the woman finds the unknown. the idiot girl always walks the path unnoticed, or the wall enclosing the last field before the mountain. dawn comes like a child wrapped in an old man's arms. the church's cobalt roof hallows a summit of purple, the cradled ravine twists in a stupefaction of blue. the house has no fevers or deception of doctrines. on a matrix of almandine a delicate blossom is created at a cry of the child. and like pale bricks for a hermit's cell the hands of the midwife attend at the birth of light. among red cloths and silver ferns, where mirrors and decanters and horsehair brushes hang, and in among the tilth where earth splits and trickles heated by the darling fallow, standing in the gold and silver of the thing unmimed, above walls and cobbles the huge flowers wave in triumph exalting the mystery of blue. green eyes murmur in the prickly beard, the words are sung with euphony. in the retina is the slowly waving corn of august, and the sun's heliotrope straightens in the prisms of air.

*

under skies dark with the sun and arms of the sea and among rocks that are very very old, i see the world through the eyes of a child. far away hills that roll in the short-lovely heat of a spring day, islands where no-one treads black with solitude, oceans gone viridian copper or a chalky gold. under closed eyelids of the dream, thick with sleep and meditation, swift shadows work, the child's mime of the world's inconsistency – a myriad of cells swarmed to a fine tilth. the wind drops in the cloudless grass and the heather lacking bones and in silent caves. it is azure and winged flight. from the sun a butterfly spreads out of its silver chrysalis, beautiful is the flower in the valley, dew in the eye of this one pale blue here or of that one yellow-white in which the doped fly lies. it is the juice of violets and yellow aconites, and the purple clouds that come finally in the evening. beautiful is the smell of rain, the shadow of the rock not even the wind can loosen, the silent caves and the winged flight ...

*

what could it have been but the idyll ! the mountain sleeping through the snow in august. yes the idyll ! in the amber sky, the stones and the sheep and the red fish, o the little trout with trout tongues, tumbled rocks seen through glass and the dream. the gnarled tree, the twisted root, the winter elms and the weir, the cliffshore walk and the descent to small bays, the demons watching the silence of the waves, the earth held in eternity's numb sway. then a sly devil scatters every veil and doubt flies in the skywheel of flame – wild fiend, old greybeard, old mad woman meeting the air with instinctive pressures, geriatric languor deceptive circus where desires bluff. the resin and the ochre and the colourful masquerade, cliffs that bury the moon, the song gathered up until it bursts in the air : the swarm of boyhood fantasies, gentle child, what told you this but the hieroglyphics on the wall and the hieroglyphics in the snow, the wren, the cow and the crow, the dance of winter flowers ? what moulded your vision the shape of astral dust, the encounter at green, the iceberg breaking, the slow procession of sheep, the agreeable book of the sea – what else but the idyll.

*

o to get up from the sickbed and walk through the green meadows after rain. fields flanked by the old past masters of this rare art and the young aspirants sticky and raw. the sky will be the colour of resin and as wet as the love we leave in our thighs. along the path by the edge of the wood, with blueberries thick in buzzing flies. very slowly we will lose our way without noticing. mosses of the darkest green release waters, bitter and silky, under our feet and fragrant juices seep up between our toes. the leaves are big red sobs and, through the branches, eyes are gleaming, and then suddenly ! we are out under a wide-open sky that is mad with the laughter of children and dressed in the gold and the crimson and the silver of clowns. and we go running off across the heath to find the green eyes that guard the lonely pond and the old gypsies who would still be drinking their thin cabbage soup.

*

a child approached the blue square. old peasants were huddled at their local wine, and shopkeepers with fleshy heads stood in the empty doorways. under calm skies madames swayed their parasols and a scent of white went up the valley towards where the languorous summer slept. the child stopped at the green gate of a presbytery : " i have come from brown shores and lakes that hum with myrtle and red fish. banners of purest white harnessed my transformation. old nomads, blinking with sleep and meditation, led their animals from blue caves and guided me along the lakes of topaz. young women passed whose bodies swayed through meadows of rank grass and lilies. i slept under walls which were embroidered in gold and embellished with filigree silver, tokens of happy summers resounding to the voices of children, toxic nerves lulled by thick warm milk. but now i am hunted to the heart of the wood of my childhood games by ravenous wolves. my tongue is torn out by a hundred thick white teeth. whips fastened with steel cornices lash my back and my eyes. the fevered spasms of old servant girls bubble terribly from me. i am seduced by intense and delirious spectres. white bones shudder against silver walls. i see the light and shadows of other worlds as if i had left the earth, visions in parables of childhood fantasy. " he passed on. the peasants had not seen, their idleness consumed in archaic gestures. the shopkeepers, the teachers, the priests had not heard, their faculties endearing skies that lacked childish sensibilities.

*

a sad corsair sets out from the gay harbour bar. at the police house a skull sits up and reads the notices on the wall. in the parks dead hyacinths converge at the ululation of gold. in the suburbs crows whirl around a hunkered girl and the unsaid rosary. beyond the walls, the deaf woman follows the path to the church shot with cobalt and angeluses die down in the starry night. at the mayor's nod children who have exposed the town's democracy are incarcerated, and model citizens traffic illegal liquor. it is undoubtedly true that blossom used to garland the womenfolk's hair and pomegranate seeds were cast towards the moon for luck. good corn waved in fields of dew but this year once again the barges are full of mouldered jams, and bees extract mustard and oxidised quicksilver from the stamens of sly foxgloves. trains hurtle in darkness and castles burn in abysses of proud grief. thirsts feast in the dust of street corners, tramps lie by the side of canals where the sun has risen out of scum and water. days of solitude in the nausea of noon heats, more dust and wildernesses and apple trees screaming in winter beside white walls, sunflowers and seeds, poppies of august and the heavy fragrance of the swayed music, and the girl who, out walking with friends, is a covenant of midnight roses and auroras and recreations, the heavy juices of the cuckoo, the nights that need no stars. who like fish swimming in mid-air will cast from themselves congealing metals or the deluded prefecture of the town ?

*

it is the savage metamorphosis and the rain. it is the rock of hidden signs. voices of the forest will be recalled in the games of childhood and there is grit in the eye, in the eye, in the vein, in the blood. spit it to the wind with an excess of vehemence. behind, an arm is nailed to the wood or it is paralysed with numbness, and turning round a hand is shivering in the limp air. is he, restraining fitful sobs, to run down to the shore and hail the boat of shame that whirls in from the channel ? the choice is not made out of necessity but the very choice made at all condemns the journeyman to his soulless wandering. hyenas bark at the sun. merchants and tramps drink of the honey that falls from the trees. at the spliced tongue of silence he prefers to sing, to consume his myth or be consumed by it. beginning with the sirens of infinite beauty the good fantasy and the pain of awakening, in heaven or in hell, and ending with the deception of bells the impossibility of movement and the pain of recollection, in the purgatory of this world. like this, it is possible to distinguish the stage-set from the ground beneath the feet, to know the footing in the breach, and plot the vertigo of falling : to be able to see fear and hold it in the breath :

the troll descending from the mountain forests, the giaour in the cloistered valleys, the tree and the skull in the gorge. in summer, horses used to sweat and in winter fish were caught through holes in the ice. now the sky is full of mud and fire. we have thrown charity from our knees.

*

journeyings during daylight hours towards the foreign city with sleeping drivers had tightened the skin of his endurance. on the last bus in from the outskirts, night was clouding the destiny of young girls and at that late hour a park or a bench or an obliging maitre d'hotel was the only hope for cold sleep. twilight blooms haunted the dreams and the drummer struck out midnight. in the morning, lapwings spired helicoils among the hayricks, and skirts of the river and starlings divided the city in topological plots. clocks and church bells rang, the sun heralded fogs. bookshops and pubs, each in a new year's cheap plenty, served amber foams (most lovely) for the array of nerves and on the bridges women hid in serge dresses (most fashionable). breads of stone ground flour and meats were to be eaten with inexpensive vegetables among bushes in the park. at midday a sky of sacred oaths plunged the city into darkness and a rain came to curse the sulking air. from limp parchment the saint spoke out in eternity's numb sway harsh reproaches for the futile sky. holiness quivered in obelisks of atmosphere. afterwards the drink and the farewell, the hostellers' night and the long homeward journey, being reduced to childish taunts by the nausea of an explored and rejected route.

*

carried his coracle to the black stones, to the shores of the water and set his coracle into the tourmaline sea. and the great still lakes of the sea lost sight of all shore. sailed on until the flags were flung across mid-morning. and set his lines and watched them. or the golden trail of the water. or the sun with amber draperies and crimson fruits, and there were apricots in his boat, which he ate and brought in fish until the sun was obscured. when a storm arose that continued for many days, he was wrecked with the ox-hide of the boat and was carried this way and that and was driven onto a shore without knowing. it was a white room, white clad women gliding by. or some honey of the worker bees. and as he fell into each dream there rose from the sea a gull on a purple sky, a symbol of peace as he left behind the fever of days.

*

bless this child in warm may winds, in the soft rains of spring an odour of lilac and pomander from the hill and the waters of midday ocherous and calm, the child walks and the hedges are full of the voices of heroes, the grasses are red albums where pages smell musty. past the weir, the white walls, the swans and the stubble, snows of deep continents. mornings in the dark wood when her eyes and laughter shimmered away, green mosses, silver fingers in the silent pond. barefoot she goes among the violets and the thick yellow haze, the sleep of her dress and the lively luck of her movement. marvellous is the smell of rain, marvellous the gentle eyes of the foal, the old man's bloodshot mirrors of childhood. cupboards secretly open and from the cupboards and her child's chest at nightfall she assembles her toys. this old wooden doll here with only a calico dress and lacking an arm, and the chalky canvas, one with the rich shawl of hair. immense is the sky with white cloud, the yellow sheets swelling in the sun by the apple grove, the warm milk of the grasses, the lilies decaying with the reeds ...

*

in the hotel rooms are the dear children with bright eyes. in the hotel rooms with water and jugs, their step on the stair tells of mornings away on the sands on the beach. in the alcove a sombre angel steps, the market-place, a sudden halting of wildcat feet. from the hillside streams pour into valleys of pine. in the thick oaks a languishing mother and far above an immense father moving his hands in reassuring arcs. through the terracotta and the evening sun sisters are eating purple grapes, their shadows falling into the firm arms of red grass. cool bars of light surround the mountain slope, caves from which white doves have flown. among the curtains are voices of woodland legends, winds deep in blue lakes, a sun on the far-off island. door dark and panelled and the knowledge she has put on and the meadows and seas and skies and the bird circling on high and the wingbeat and the staggering minute and the held breath and the oceans that sink away as if a stopper, as large as the sky, had been released in the neat full sea.

*

on one side of the dream is the yellow flower, an incarcerate who believes he will walk again. and on the other side a dead angel from a dead sun. jasmine and purple inhabit the breach, on one side the green box and the child, the dodecahedron and the wind. and on the other the sea and the stars, every era since the oceans were violet and the lands black, the sea and the stars and the uncertain horizon. the inhabitants say, " here is a beginning of salt water " and " here the wind bounces through ". in this bubble every drunken acrobat, every tubercular clown, and swaying rope. and there, entranced by the shimmer on the inverse side of the membrane, the mother and the child. a savage meteor will wreck the crystal and capsule of this world. in one segment of the diaspora, the new philosophy, the cardinal number and its indeterminacy, the quintic equation and the quanta. and in the reciprocal swarm, the maelstrom of colours (each one and its possible extension grown as a tree) and the metamorphosis. and the inhabitants say, " oh someone speaks to me ! I do not know how to answer. i have never been talked to before " and " marvellous, we can give you an especially light walrus flipper " and " foxes ? who, me ?

oh no ! it happens that a very poor hunter is present ". the long talks, the laughter, the people wandering in at all hours of the day and night. there is another side to this house where the reeds blow above a lake and pine trees dance in ribbons like breton women's caps. and the mountain lacks savagery because the inhabitants live with it. on this side the unrepeatable waves and the harbour wall and on the other the flight over pointed trees the outlines that lose their detail and the crust of the earth. here violet sands and copper seas and there a sky of silver ochre and haunted blue. where the one world ends a dark chamber, an oracle, and a box, and where the other one begins a silence as of the birth of crows and the desperate happiness of that house.

*

dawn wrapped in cold chiffon knelt beneath disoriented pillars of the sun. the servant ran out for the gelding among the white mists. the yellow flower was dancing in the stillness of the day. summer smiled at the disinclination of the inhabitants to wander past the divinely regarded canyon. in the alpine meadows cows' bells rang. the rider set out on his journey into the trance of legends and unexpected winds turned him towards the untreadable regions ...

*

evening brought rain and turned the sky to amber, the heather to blue, and the grass to multi-coloured rags. oceans swelled into the silent sea and the earth-flower drank up the sun. the man on the scaffold recaptured the hours of his childhood bliss. the summoned people left at the onset of the purges and the precast water towers collapsed in the city. a mine shaft whirred and then caved into the earth with lagoons and stars and pneumatic snows. in the village a blacksmith struck out iron rails for the war and peasants heard of wonderful victories from abroad. in the sanatorium the sweetheart drank milk with her fingers and made curious rhythms with her arms. in the desert camels announced in manifold harmonies their chronic discontent. in the palace the dwarf princess was turned to a stem of rare beauty much to the king's relief and suitors brought her a gown of sky blue silk and black sables. in the lake a flower opened its eyes and drank in the dew. a child walked back to the shore. petrified steps were stamped along the railway as if soldiers were storming a redoubt, as if a soul were storming a soul. and then the dark dance followed, as implicitly as if four dead angels had ridden out the storm.

*

it was commanded he leave the palace and break through the sanctuaries. that he run along the boulevards faster than the transport carts and make a passage through the crowds of stubborn bodies. this he did. he was told to leave the city behind, the first meadows and the skulls that are quarried for stone, that he was to do nothing unless specifically ordered. he came to roads cut deep through fields of corn and streams where rushes grew up onto the path, trout in small ponds and blue deer under trees and stubble worked to a fine tilth. he came to huts among trees and atmospheres the breath of dead monks, landscapes of green boxes and burning shadows and prisms of air. he passed beneath silk screens and saw a young woman climbing a narrow stone stair and a child with a calm eye. he passed rings of flesh and dark chambers and jasmine shagged with frost and he saw people huddled together in nights of shooting and sudden lights. he saw stadia of internment and ghetto guards and horizons of random flaring. he saw torsos growing upwards like petrified trees and airs gone orange with blight. he saw bones merging with the colours of snow and gang trains travelling to frozen seas and trucks and shacks and barbs and outer walls. he saw beaches dusty with age and bright pools, blue phantoms and frosted trees and early crabs, towers and outhouses and machine guns. and suddenly ! the creation of the rose with the thorn and a fraying of the world loosened into hurdy-gurdy silence.

he had visions walking on the edge of dreams. and the dreams fell away and the pain was annulled with pain. whatever crushed him he blessed with incense. he had the keys to the great mysteries and immortal encounters. he had music in his house, in his hands. one tap from his fingers brought the world breathing to the rhythms of his heartbeat. children called on him to make clear waters fall out of the sun. citizens urged him to overcome their fates and he was brought libations and garlands, and cherries and apricots. he did not sacrifice music. he turned his head this way and that and there were new loves, he closed his eyes and men rose up in every part of the city and the sun was their silver banner, the moon their yellow brocade. he understood the significance of the supplications and the prayers for the healing of pain and he made the slogans sing softly. he knew the great deserts of the city and the people thirsting under copper suns and the petitions and assemblages, the endless discussions and marches down wide roads, the derelictions and festivals and the wild shouts burnt into the nights, these things he understood and he made them deaths in fruitful flowering. he took things in his hands and the world was burnt away.

*

in the night trees' shade, in the laughter of their solitude, they are found. they believe in pure circuses and trophies of light and the masquerade festivities of the sea ! they believe that the sun has a horror of moving stone, of the usurping of its self-created energy. they believe that their dancing girls destroy themselves like fireflies in the pure blue dawn. from the buried treasures came the will of the king and the apocryphal biographies and from the sealed grottoes came the talismans and the chosen words and the annals of the law. from the yellow islands came the chronicles and a knowledge of the sea and the prophecies of sadness and joy, and the great calm of the oceans listens to the people, and the people listen to the seas and the nights need no stars.

*

does it begin with the lapse between the unrepeatable waves and the crows in the small harbour town, with the brown evening and the golden flower in the snow mountain ? does it begin with the children out hunting among the sands and the old men along the shore and the blue phantom of summer ? does it hover into the sky until the details lose their intensity and black spots appear ? do the hems split and the skirts shrink and the buttons burst off ? does it flow down with silver from the hills and does it set out from the marble quay destined for the three islands in the bay and on the other side of the sun ? does the ice sing where it goes ? are the visions scattered and the trials ended, do the gentians flower in november, is the fly in the flower of the primrose doped, does it fall away at every edge and abyss ? are the surfaces unsure so that it plummets into the sky stained with resin ? are there lavas and auroras in the cave or moons and jackals ? does it pick among the seaweeds for mushy insects and scratch out molluscs from the muds and cast juicy starfish on the rocks ? does it collapse the groynes and urge on the million waves and make stacks out of arches ? does it arise from the bench and leave for the country ? does it pass the headlands and cross the plains and reach the chalky walls of the city ? the clock strikes, the bell rings out, the factory whistles. does it begin in the streets of long suffering with the sickening descents, does it end with the new world and the dead red waves of the sea racing in under the sun ?

*

so it's off to the station where no-one'll follow and the one-track-line to the north. a moment in the kitchen, a mouthful of tea and then tie the sky up with string – there's not even time for that. we'll leave them all behind, we'll scatter all the streets, we'll rush through the dawn chorus and the horizons ! a calmness will sustain us along the carp's hurt backbone and where the rail link ends we will continue north by foot. pillows of turf will be provided and sudden flowers and the sky will foster its thin wafers. and each new sky that we greet will make us a gift of its ligament until the yeast of the world is stained into the breadsong of dawn.

*

there is still food to eat, a last meal before leaving, the only bread for two days, and the good smell of peat. to sit for a moment at the open door, to look again at the four islands and the sky coloured amber and saffron, to warm scones on a hastily done up griddle, to know that snow is threatening – islands of cliffs under the aegis of cooling lavas, to take up the rucsac, turn over the embers and with hands laden walk the four miles to the road. snow will (already) be falling, and not a white curtain for the night but a whole oasis of grey and mauve memories, as if swift shadows were stamping through a desert. no matter in the short northern afternoon. to get to the crofter's welcome and the top room where the window panes are crushed ice. to brew tea on the gas lamp. to leave the black cliffs behind. to throw a fleece cap on the fence. with the moon in the snow at midnight, it's almost as light as day. to know about candles and the birth of crows, the mountain understands such foibles. (to know) bone is the new-born crow. and i am still the same man and inside is the neat full sea. the rocks, winds divide over them. barefoot on the june heather or the frozen march moss in shoes hung together with string, and a plug of black tobacco wouldn't go amiss. time for a short walk among the moor crests before the boat leaves for the other side of the sea, from the eastern side of the western island, and the train that will have to wait for the ships.

*

(will you be king,) will you be king with your tattered tongue (and sandals) standing (on your chair) in the middle of the dear room ? sunrise clothed you in the dark wings of a starling, in branches of willow and late gold, and the voices of children hum in the leafless grass. will you be queen, will you be queen standing by the great austere cave block wall ? you spoke me words no-one else knew, you rang bells until milk slipped from the copper mountain. you recognised the sun by the resin in the rough pastures and antelope began to graze across the sullen waters. rain fell on the iron roof. in a dram-glass a bluebell stem the colour of rubbed bronze. inside the petal violet, and outside blue on blue. and the tiny white heart the odour of a curdled sea. beneath the water a leaf changes shape. outside the door small brackens uncurl and shadows are blown all across the floor. and in the strangeness of those days dawn came, wrapped like a child in an old man's arms.

*

between the tomb lies the little box, green and wooden and four-sided. between the tomb. eternity sleeps out on the roof and white doves peck. from under the ground they sense the august light and the wave that dances in the shade. a stranger shuffles by, eye full of the saliva of dogs, soul on fire near the city wharves, a yellow circle snowing portents of distension. rainbows have moved off towards geysers of copper. between the stones of the ocean his hands are becoming more clumsy. this door is for the dead. from what vault are the high flying birds called out and the murmured reticence fast gone ? the women do not sing and the sky and sea are in requiem. stars of the ocean batten down sea sands of billowing treasure. only the dead may forgive. only the dead, under a haze of cooling metals. between the tomb lies the little box, between the tomb where eternity sleeps out on the roof. now the dead saints need only arrive and he will be the emissary of the lost sun.

this time, haunted one, it will be done. the first smoke has followed your flickering, in place of the lost sun. you are no longer human. under gas towers and tall chimneys, to whom do they pray ? three blind women are sat in a couch, garbed in bloodstained cloth : they sing " i dream of my son the captured king. " in the old quarters there are children crying. what allowance is there in these songs for the sparseness of gorse ? do you hear the fireflies and see the eyes of wildcats separating ? the maimed king, reciting the nameless, rode by a forest and the moon shone clear. by shored up channels he saw their chieftain spread his fingers wide : he, the dead one, his face will glow. petrified city, do you see the sun or hear the island that is growing in its seas ? a litany of skies in the mute treasuries among the stunned fish. how is he to bury you, sun-city, betrayer, shadow seized by evening ? your beauty haunted the flood and pursued the things we cannot know. the first creatures are passed. flicker in place of the abandoned sun. do not look at me like that. you have been where the sea captures death with fire.

III.

'The Birds' and Other Poems

from The Conversation With Dante

One day the footsteps climbing the stair were mine.
"I knew that was you coming up the gyre," Dante said,
 opening the door to me before I had even pressed the bell
"who else would come this high with the lifts out of order.
Come in. Come in. I've been expecting you, come in ..."
And he bade me enter his cluttered and muttering home.
"Look, this is the canzone on the shelf here, the one that
you've been searching for without knowing what it was.
Among all the ledges of dust and papers. I will run
 my fingers along the manuscript edges and parchments
starched with juices and age to show you. Come, come."
And he took me to a hidden back room lined with papers.
"Here it is, the canzone ! You can see it is made up of
 a sequence of almost identical stanzas. It is about life
 in your city, that guard-dog palace of gated tenements,
the stricture of small fanatic gangs and ordinary people.
It is about the consigning of language to silence, not a
pure white of calm, but rather that augured abyss where
reality freezes. I know well enough how you must feel,
dissident in your democracy as I was in mine. And I am
an exile again, as I was before, like the many others
                that established time has denied ..."

                            * * *

"Sometimes what you say," I said to him "makes me think
 of the world as a jar of mushrooms that have been dried
and preserved : retaining their goodness to be extracted.
And so much of an essence is concentrated in what you

say, a palm-full being enough to steep an integral world. The power of certain words peoples me with passionate knowledge, a jet of understanding in the taste of praxis. I think you've come from an altogether other way of life bringing with you filled jars of mushrooms and honeys. Think of a sea-shore, not with the scale and tightness of burst oceans, but with the minute sovereignties of algae. Some words are like the formation of colour or lichen, pools edged with brown and green, sands & tiny shells, parts of rams' horns and skulls and stone in cold mud. Or I think of cooking soups from onion and tomatoes that I never now do in this city, skinned & simmering in water bubbled with pepper. Words that may be the tar and freshness of what we are and do, fine red algae that swarm about the tired democracies of our kidneys, subtle relieving debits for the economies of our blood, energy bundles of phonemes."

* * *

Then Dante said : "This is a dream I recurrently have about tower blocks : that they rise up in the cool night and tread across the horizons in their pastel gowns beyond the limits of the city. And it seems to me they are still asleep and walking, that they may never stop. Where do they get to and what do they do ? And how shyly they return ! What changes overcome them as they repossess the harsh and male arrogance of their daytimes. I cannot really imagine that people live in tower blocks when I see them high in the air, despite that I am living in one myself. I reckon they can be bisexual, tower blocks. Or they have the inspiration

to exchange clothes, the clothes of men and women,
tower blocks, much as women and men freely may.
To change : to be so much the same and yet wholly
different ! What must it feel like, a jumpy arrogance
in the belly ? What is it like to be a man, a woman ?
What is it like to be human down to the very bone ?
The afterward of a woman on my body, or I on hers.
Or the ordinary terrible hungers of an unfed human.
Do the tower blocks go off at night to look down on
us like ancient gods, to see the real distributions of
human hungers as we never can ?"

* * *

"But forget the dream," I said to Dante – "A friend
of mine – a teacher and mountaineer – told me he
was shaving one morning early and saw poised in
his mirror the image of a man standing on a balcony
rail about to fall. Before he'd turned round he knew
what was happening. I did not know the brain could
move at such superb but appalling speeds or how
soon a brain can be destroyed, an eye's art be erased.
Motion measured not by seconds or distance, but by
images taken in by the eye, by actions of brain cells
on other brain cells, by the rush to speak of blood.
And he told me also that a cormorant had flown in
through the shut window of his seventeenth floor.
Cormorants have been breeding two or three years
now in the derelict docks 'til they were dispersed.
One had disoriented its flight and swerved through
the large plane of glass of a tower block in Poplar.
This man woke suddenly to scuffing black wings

and eyes in the next room. Strangely the bird was
alive, its bloodless beak pointing eastward to seas,
and he let it through the shattered window until it
fell then gained an equilibrium and then flew off.
I did not know cormorants flew that high above
the surfaces beneath them."

* * *

"I cannot envisage where the city ends, if it does,
nor do I retain the returned ellipses of sight. I keep
thinking of my mother and her face, imagining
she is calling me. But that is something different.
The city is like a woman is, or a man : you open
the shoulder of the city and take out a measure of
wheat, a word cluster, the closed shoulders show
no sign. And what two things could be less alike :
the little word clusters in the brain and the leap of
terror there also ? And of the leap of sheer joy ?
This mimesis between word and world obsesses me.
On clear nights it seems the city will be submerged.
The sea will rise up and the sky become a container
of clear water. Will anything at all have changed ?
Will life continue like this on the immersed floors ?
I shall eat mango and cut jackfruit portions and my
country will remain tolerant, but of its rabid dogs
and not its varied peoples. All this I can see as in a
lucid dream, or when from an open glider and past
its edge there's nothing until the exact land laid
out down there so precisely."

"Tell me this, Dante, and tell me what to do.
I have lived three years alone, my university and
scuola semantica, in a house at the edge of an island.
The sea was on one side, moors went away behind.
I've lived in an old cottage with my wife and an old
lady over eighty, a cottage without mains light or
hot water, cottage caught in a hill among sand works
with a path curling through small strawberry garden.
I have lived in a small room high in a tower block,
in a small room with Punjabis overlooking a yard,
in a room big as its bed with an annexe for cooking
and white jasmine out the back window by the wall,
in houses by busy roads and in places of utter silence.
The first house of my almost-life had walls three feet
thick and tiny windows. Now I am in a city in a thin-
walled flat with glass stretched the whole block. I
have found myself here in this city, streets of slanted
brightnesses and the sun-pocked river, inside the
intestines of the city and I follow people around. I
do not understand this preoccupation with law and
order, this flaunting and dis-knowledge of justice.
What is vision or ellipsis from a window or an eye ?
I follow people around I do not know in this city
with its humours of decay."

* * *

"Have you noticed," he answered "the details
in Piero's 'Nativita' ? The water bottle beneath
the shepherd's seat, the ladder across the back wall
of the barn, the simple patterns on the hems of the
garments, the sparse plants with three small birds
among them, the jay of the roof, the empty street
of the town behind that's climbed by seven houses.
Yet the figures hold their rightful places, are in such
marvel of balance : details we love for doing just that.
I wandered one day into a gallery in the city's centre
and there it was, luminous door to our punctured lives.
It put so much of my mind back to that other life !
Who are those singers damaged even as we are, yet
perfect, and perfect only in their damage ? Who are
they put there floating on solid earth among black
plants and mute birds in their singers' almost trance ?
Quietly but firmly you approach this painting and it's
as if most ordinary paintings can only bruise us, and
you come to a temple and are drenched in porticoes,
in columns of light. How is it the columns became
singers with stringless instruments with you outside ?
and everything is found in space, suffused and then
measured by depth. A shepherd is pointing toward
the edge of sight : the golden ladder of Piero's
                          canvas."

                          * * *

"Yes, it is like that," I said "It is like that. You
want to know that man, the one sat there with his
foot on his knee, that woman with her arms akimbo,
and that one whose thigh marks the movement of
her skirt. You know the city smells of apricot and
sweetcorn because at dawn you have tasted them.
And you know there is shame and you know there is
no shame. You feel certain people jut out from the
surface of the earth, that they stand in a red-golden
atmosphere close by small crystal piles of speech
and blood and that this is more real than any news
bulletin or placard or banner or sharp investment.
You know this and you want to say it : you want
to say these things in a world where such things
are not said. You know that is one part anyway
of being a poet. And you'd like to paint them, to
pain them with words. Those with fleshy hair or
big outstretched hands. The young who've aged
with heavy macs on warm days, old women who
stop close to bus-stands wrapped in their nerves.
You want to talk with them – but how do words
describe ? To sit with them and listen to the little
blood piles of speech. I want to make this known
again as part of life – it is the only logic I can
understand – that once again salt may be able
to speak through our bones, sugars through
                    our bloods."

'All the weight of the sun and the city ...'

All the weight of the sun and the city
then tepid water that neither warms nor cools.
Think of the fragrant herbs of speech, they are
no longer accessible. Lovely stems and flowers
in their own places come through springy turf.
My mouth cannot reach these words now, neither
can I warm the touched mouths of other people.
Nothing like the certainty of bulbs breaking to
their own colours through impalpable chance.
Or the grace of friendship, that now is lost.
My mind is like a moss floor churned by diggers.
I cannot walk there any more, I cannot touch
the cool plants of morality with acute words.
The sands they kept on scooping out were the
fibred tensions of my own mind and candour.
Now that hill is levelled, it is taken away and
dust roads enclose a home and flower garden.
All the weight of the sun and city pelts down
in thickening air and through the dense liquids
cranes swing above shells and broken structures.
In the scooped edges there my soul is measured
by the dirt lines and archaeology of the earth.

Sadie's Story

I, Sadie, an ordinary dazed woman, out of figure
and middling in age step out into the colour world.
Huge gulps of air and dust knock me about as I go
to the girls at the launderette not sparing laughter.
But then the mechanic comes and turfs us in round
the drier : all of life wrinkles up through the guts
and pulls us about without ever washing us clean.
There's the twist : we'll be knocked about the same.
I'll be tossed onto the slab and gutted and given
the chop. The cook'll come and slap me down at the
hot-plate and I'll frizzle up and be gobbed and done
to a mattie residue : I'll go to the girls the same.
Mynah birds in the market's what we are or big hunks
of pet kidneys, purple aubergines or thick cabbage ;
varied as the stuff we buy we are, and so handled.
Time enough I'll spend splayed out again though,
before I end laid up by a different stiff ... And so
I, Sadie, thinking of the coloured world and fast
roads, will go out into the horny winds, buffetted
spun and hung dry, engrossed in the spitty weathers
and crushing my bubs against the grainy bone of God.
Maybe he will take my diddies and the hidden white of
calyx and my marrow and come, to his huge and quiet
hands, the white hidden where still I manage to sing.

'The heart of my decade has been ripped out ...'

The heart of my decade has been ripped out
the middle years and my divided mind.
If I were to imagine the city pale as air
the weeping streets would be submerged.

We are here beneath a sea and no longer the
singular neurosis that brought us to its shore.
I watch the dark static shapes arrive and
know that rescuing night will not now come.

So many worlds tear us apart and what gives
light makes it painful to attain. If I were to
rip out my backbone, to rip out the middle years,
it would not provide a highway or meridian of
warmth.

We are here where sea is always sea and it is
beneath a black angelic sun within the city.
The heart of the years has been torn out and
burnt, but the sacrifice was only cruel.

It is not black despair or the song's sadness
it is the panic and dark sessions of sleep let
into our flesh, but I would have loved to have
heard a golden stream of words engendered
by my world.

The Birds

The scalloped wren fearfled in at the blue
open door later almost than the last second.
And the kestrel that had swerved to avoid hut's
rock staggered in the constant wind with only
the shadow of the tiny bird in its craw beak.
To have lost prey so close to the ground!
The hunter swivelled in the balance of the
beating wind and the brain lobes that moved its
wings, then rose again to survey the ground.
The amazed wren was safe in a new void of
stone. It fluttered and stormed in confused
terror, not being able to get back to the
shore rocks, the easy wrack of the unfelt sea.
What had a kestrel been doing diving a wren?
Then the other birds began to arrive, keen
to confer on this different world. And the
desperate struggle of the birds was begun.

The Island

I remember the lovely island in my mind.
At one time the earth was a lovely island
we floated in, even if the realities of life
were more ambiguous, gratifying and unsure.
We inhabited what was a lovely place, not
just a recess from which the anabasis came.
Now our earth is by us changed ; at first
it was a matter of people becoming islands.
Later there were not sufficient people or
islands to matter. As long as there is a
lovely place the earth has retained its
dignity. But if there are no islands we
are a cold apostrophe of dust. The mountain may return to its intense first heats
flow flat on ground we will have destroyed.
I remember the lovely island in my mind.
It was with flowers torn in early summer,
its birds manoeuvred in the unburnt air.

For Sorley MacLean

I have seen dogs in your poetry
A wild sustained clatter that dappled the snow
              with paw prints
Dogs that trample the crisp herbs of what is said
I remember it was a hallway of roaring waves
and outside a grey spittle of weathers
Time held repeated in the blue rooms of the sea
I have seen your dogs in these dead days
Trampling the fresh herbs of speech
And you taught them to do that
Wanting to keep not pets but animals of necessity
It is not that you are remote from us
We do not understand
But your language is too close to the music
              of how things are
Your calm house built round with silent weather
I have seen your words like good sheep dogs
biting to whistle on a waned hill
And running close as a bird's shadow to the slope
From the high clusters of the rock faces
You are bringing the wild ones down
And a whole word-horde moves off the quick heats
of the edge down to the fank-trodden crispness
So you trample the clean herbs of what is said
Isn't that how it must be, Sorley ?
Poetry has the dog and deer, brother lamb and crow
And speech is a skull flecked with soft wools.

From William Ross's 'Òran Eile'

The wounds of my eaten soul are
not healed by joy or by grief;
my story is let loose everywhere
everywhere people tread it to dust.
Daylight does not now unfold
to me the glory you once were.
Joy is gone down spired sun-cliffs
in the lowlands of autumn leaves.

Vision of fast streaming hair!
Lost angel! I call but in vain.
May the soon sprung rose of my clay
flower on your sunny garden wall.
Your sea-journeyings have flattened
me, hung me on thorns; I am a
soldier at the edge of the strife,
bleeding, wayward and unknown.

Parting threw wide open the gates
on our bitter flood of tears
and has left me, runt among stags
of good breeding, despised.
It would have been better had I been
reared deaf senseless blind; not
knowing the beauty that burns and tears
or the sensations that craze my mind.

You will hear little good of me
from cynics who talk of my ills.
" A poet! Spinner of dreams
vain, hopeless, without direction. "

My people carved farms from the
hill's flanks in the lumbering years
broke horses with their will's power.
I sing through sunlight and water.

Though summer flings wild petals
grief has no such payment in it ;
there is no welcome from struck music
or the laughter of playing children.
My footsteps do not ring now
on windy days in the high hills.
My feet fall and cling on the round
lowlands under where the mountain
                    falls.

Ashes And Diamonds

The blizzard that came was not
      a narrowing in the spirit.
If language is a game, freedom
was trapped inside and all the
colours erupted into silence

In the internment there was enough
      of hunger cold and gangrene
And out from the coal shafts were
lifted the human bodies of the
         dead

Kuroń and Michnik were imprisoned.
      Workers in
      Gdansk, Katowice killed.
The dance of time has now become
      a frozen music

A sacrifice was made that was not
just cruel and ignorant. Ashes were
mixed in with diamonds with neither
      shape nor taste.
Ice rattles, the requiem of the word

The blizzard that came was not a
      blizzard in the spirit.
The struggle that seemed likely was
crushed, the people reduced to
      this sacred limp

Palach

We are put in mind of Palach, of
fire that is potent but put to the use
of despair. There are enough Palachs
in every part of the world and the
master of tongues can no longer
speak.

John MacCodrum At Eubhal

It's two hundred year since you died there
              & the people
off the mountain were cleared to Canada &
New England, Cape Breton & Vancouver
          the way of all islanders

You saw the start of that clearance, people
          put from their homes, not
by necessity but by the new luxury of others
an old order breaking down to a newer
          one far worse

What does it mean to you, the sea that takes
          in the varied streamings of life,
the sea that spat out people off their tongues,
the sea set against our unremitting breath
          our cogent speech ?

Someone stood on the edge of a lucid shore
          & cursed the stupid, patriarch sea
the sea of Manrique, the sea of Cardenal &
Pablo Cuadra's inland sea. Someone stood
          cursing on the edge of the sea

You were born out at Aridh an Runnair by
      the edge of Comgan's churchyard,
at Hogharry out by Griminish near to where
white crests cruise in from St. Kilda on the
      tilt of the swelling sea

The mountain still lies there cruising in its
      stillness. Did you know
it had been a huge vessel broken down slowly
by four thousand million years of sea-crash
      battering its yardage ?

The sea is a thin soup with gristle-floats
      for islands, the Cuillins rising
beyond its rim like a strop-blade ready to
plunge through a stubble of tired hands.

You who were born in sight of the throbbing
      ocean, what did you not know of
fickle unconsciousness, of diamond bodies, of
black holes coursing with spilt energy in the
      ur-physics of our earth ?

The pricked needles of Heisker & Causamul
      wove in & out your mind &
fashioned of your townships a warp & weft,
a cartologer's respite against the deadpan
      of archive.

Wherever you go on Uist, you cannot escape
the sea, but some places among
the gneiss hummocks sink you straight down
through hot unscoured origins to the memory
zones below

All your life the sea was following you : Paible,
Tigharry, Ronay, Langass, Eubhal.
It crashed down from big houses battering raw
waves across shorelines of people.

You voyaged from Tigharry's machair to the
far side of Eubhal :
the land was stiffened sea & the whole universe
was contained in a small circle of stilled water.

And the red ball – the sun's red fever ball –
sizzled the dazed air & came
rolling over you in one moment of intolerable
speed & another of unendurable slowness,
until our whole earth melted.

You thought your communities had gone from
one slow purgatory to another
& it took two hundred years. You went through
the bouncing coast & it took a moment's speck
beneath the lucid sun.

You must take yourself out on the moor now
        under an opaque silent sky
& move about in the rocks' stiff seas. All is ash
& colour but you are not thinking about that.

The mountain has begun to melt & the perfect
        curve globs down in thickets.
All is calm & colour, the sky flesh-coloured &
        grey-blue under time's white sutra.

And I can see you there on the other side of
        the mountain, the ruins north
of Loch a' Gheàdais & Bàgh Mòrag take on a
used look, become full with new thresholds
        of curtailed speech.

And I can see you walking by the Minch coast
        just where the cormorants
shat the lake cliff white in early summer & fat
gulls waddled on the edge of an old-new world

If you were to go this day to the other side
        passing the hill at its lowest point,
getting to the far & turquoise shore : in place
        of people – a bog filtered out to the sea.

Cold Januarys & Julys in the moaning winds
    you put your land on your shoulders
like a cloak, colour of moss & crottle, & you
    walked in the driven rain.

I look back at you from two hundred years : in
    the deep places of my mind
a knowledge forms that time – there is no time –
walks on this edge never falling. We just fall
    through the cylinder time.

My mind goes as complex as the petrology of
    those schist bands – all the
hypersthenes, the horneblendes – & as simple
as a rock with the egg of the oyster catcher
    caught in its palm

We the rivers journeying under an idiot sun.
    We the seas
withholding mountains with our blood. We
the birds eating & shitting on matter earth.
    O poor mother of us all !

And I'm thinking of the earth as diamond body.
    Broken atom. Irreverent rock. Black
point that glows over with spilt energy. We who
    collapse down the cylinder time.

Speech is lovely. The absence of speech is pain.
Speech is pain, the absence of
pain is silence. But silence's absence is blood
pulsing through a body that can move
into pure constriction.

And I can see you moving on the rock wastes.
Sea is the distance moved in
one lifetime. You moved from Paible to the far
side of Eubhal. Though it wasn't far, it was
through a vanished world ...

Visions

who can lead us to the table the water or
            the grave ?

                        churches ?
                bread and wine reconstitute
                            the body ?

            in suffering
        in anguish and in silence
                there is strength
            and in the sounds
                of a silent age

dead fish in the air swimming
        and the heron at the bottom of the lake
    towards the mountains of the Altai
            move,
        and there, appearing above
                them,
            Bulgarian peasants dance

                            we are here in the
                                solitude, affirming

we are sensual men
        we understand the bearing of gifts and the faces
            and the women of wide ways

but who can lead us to the table
        the water or the grave ?

reindeer in Mongolia ?
islands and other lovely places ?
the songs of old Vienna ?
in Iceland the farmer rides
north into the moors
and an Irish monk in a bark
arrives

reindeer there are, white,
and towers of silence
and in Finnmark also
where spruce trees snow dust up
on high wing

and we are far from home
and must watch
the enduring seas

it is not time yet

in the meridian life, in
the zenith of suns
they issue forth
as if from Samarkan to the Atlantic seaboard
banners of azure were the sky and
songs of sorrow the sea

o you skies of amber vision
you striped mares of the steppe
clouds that buffet the corded silks
you
golden vessels
and icons of gneiss
what resins caution your bloodrush

through the azure
what low buzz of prayer is caught
on the world's wide winds ?

                    it is not time yet to sing
                          but under their
                          speckled domes
                    the fat fish jump

who can know the water from the grave ?

                                    i
                          or you ?
                    but it is good to touch
                    & none can endure
      alone

            in Siberia the taiga ends
                  suddenly at rivers & roads
            and muds are churned into ruts

(but who can tell the table from the water
            or the grave ?)

      grandmothers stroke their darlings'
            hair with blossom
                  or with the silence
            of the milk of their eyes –
      they are enthralled – but who can take us
            to the blessed dead ?

                    the Kara-Korum, the Gobi
                    towards the power of the sun
                          in the garden of the darkening

sea, in the light garden of the
king

or higher where the golden ladder reaches
that after climbing we must
let fall back to earth

i can just see in a haze of cold blue
the western ocean off Kerry,
the beehives of the hermits,
and there, in purple wreath,
as if thorns,
the coastline of Lanka
Marco Polo on roads
of chalcedony and jasper
Francis Xavier hearing legends
of bronze plains

Cook, Magellan and the dark
side of the sun

and
so the old woman becomes mad
mad the
mother of the Pope, in her
womb the Emperor of China
an Aztec priest
at her feet of clay

in the heat she left
the City of Y
and came to the City of X
of the rest there was nothing beautiful
the mosaic was red

red the bloodstones
                    and she remembers nothing
        from then on
tonight she will sleep with the
        song on her lips

                                        and she is fire,

    fire

                                                and

bright hope

            tossed in sails of ragged canvas
                muffled above the estuarine muds
            the face is lit up with a
                    last phrase of regal lassitude
                        and they are crushed now
        and talk of clouds or flowers
                                or churns of wool,
                    the lucid and diffident, along
                    wet highways, into sudden
                        shoals of water

                        where did it begin ?

                            the Kalahari
                                    or
                            the winds' wide paths,
                    voices that travel, swift
                        shadows worked
                                    to a fine tilt,
                        memory's myriad

    swarm of

                        childhood tears ?

not Alexander not Ivan not
    even Napoleon brooding over the
valley's map
    dreamed of such worlds

        was it her or you or me ?
                words in the womb ?
          red forests, a matrix of
            bone, unruffled river,
              splintered moon,
                  calm countenance

  was it in winter or in
the spring that did not come that
      we set out ?
and the absence of tundra flowers
    or the islands shimmering
      on a dark sun
that caused us to stop and listen ?

        close by the promontories
          but hard to grasp
      is the lonely sound of the sun
        it chars and burns
      therefore a fireball must have
      exploded, calyx crimson,
            far out there

who taught us language ?

            Genghis Khan ?

Tamurlaine ?
      each icon of Andrei
        Rublyev ?

Spitzbergens in April ?

what thin echo of the world's

contagion ?

    the sound of the sun is a joy
        to the dead, for sea is the
      edge of sight / i saw
        a man with a yellow eye
  cry out with dead delight /
          only the drowned here can die
      and only the dead good
can doubt

                we see out there
            sirens by stormed skerries
              singing their joys at the
           things we cannot know

  and he was mad that man with his
      rubric hair, maddened by the
    sound of the sun
      red spheres redden and the rocks cry out
  with fierce tears the rocks cry
    to see a man with a yellow eye
        dancing on a sea of light

          it is sweet to the nostrils
          the islands to the west
        the islands & the worker bees
          the combed honeys & the cowls
            of silence

and the white peacock of the
spheres

who taught us language ?

and the huts brightly coloured
with hope

now departed, the mercenaries
from the Alps
and we are alone

the spider will try to hide
in its web

we are here in the solitude from
which many have gone who
cannot return
we are here in
the solitude affirming,
and you also, dead

on wings of snow

for some it is strength, for
some the order of the world

men down mines, children
of whom loved ones
sing

and the beautiful women stepping out
on their way to the sun

charred, charred and
charred, charred
and burnt
and across the seas are gentians
of snow

a drunken tiller water and wine
lets loose a sun more silver
and transparent glazes
thicken the sky

island in the sun
what vertigo lightens
your summer of darkness
into your summer of day ?

who watches over us now ?

silence is the language
white haired grandmothers
caress young children with

day
day and the rich earth
that send roots into the air ?

a drunken soul stomps
down the railway track between
sleepers of thick snow

the tundra of last days ?
the flowers of worn down sanity ?
a final palisade to which to cling ?

in Greenland glaciers break
                into the sea

                                        pollen from Novosibirsk

                        the goat paths of Italy, Greece the
                        darling, the yellow tilth,
                        marble crust, sanctuaries of rock

            who watches now ?

                                                    the
                                                no-one
                                                breathing
                                        the nothing that is

        ruts descend from the plateau
    and close by women are heard
                and there is a sacred place
        often covered by salt water
    streams flow from the other side
                of the mountain
        and from the tower-top also
    where people do not like
                    to go

                        westward are the cliffs
                        beyond the mountains

    from love of music the
            clusters of juice growth repose
                        and straightens
                                the little path

    the wayward song

in the meridian life
in the rich vein of grief

then from love of music the clusters repose
and the sun loves the youthful slugs
betokening temperance
and straightens the greening stalks

in the meridian life
in the zenith of suns
in the blind field
with the sense of the sea's being near
beech & birch
and the sense of the sea's being near
and the sea is nervous
and nervously chants

they love that music
who stand in the sight of the sun

whatever crushes you
dress it in incense
in a solemn quietness
and bow into the autumn
wind

for much the prickly head loves
to lie on the breast
by the pendant of the slanted ear

or to lie inside the loved one
and know the colours of the sea

immutable breath travels

and the world's winds deepen
into wild blue

shall we climb on ever more high
when we wake on the marble slab
and sit up in the tomb in the sky
and walk the few yards from the skull
and crawl the few years from the womb
and look past the few friends in delight
and skip the few whorls to the tomb ?

did we die or are we not dead ?
shall we climb through the blood to the sun
and twirl banners of snow round our heads ?

lift our heads
to hear the sound of the sun
the echo of bronze in the
dark spaces
the white swallows
in the sails of silence
the starling gong
in the aching bronze

and i see
light cities
and northern seas
and islands like sharks' teeth
waters mantled in their own saffron
and oceans
churned to luminous
sand

this the dark arbiter of our sanctity showed
                                        and rivers of bright

magmas & coals

language coming as an eruption
                    of shattered heats & blind vanishings
                                        along great causeways of stone

            or as gong sound in the petrified
rock forests of deserts

                                thus is the world accomplished
                                    and the lavas of vision subside
                                    and the sky but a dim smudge

                                                Kamchatka

Tierra del Fuego

                                Karakorum

            the heights of
            Machu Picchu

                                and floors inlaid with gold
                                    across the bronze causeways

here the pumice collapses
                    and no other words permeate
                                        the breath of fire ...

IV.

The Blue Bag

A Song For David Silver

Between his two eyes and the back of his skull –
    a sea that roars against calmness.
And right in the middle of his forehead – a third
    eye, where the electricity of this world
        can get through

A hidden hole where the forceps had made a grab
    towards the tired womb of his mother.
Since he was pulled out he's had to endure doctors
    and diagnoses, pills and the neutering
        threats of this world

One time he rang my door at six in the morning :
    "hello, I've come for sugar."
So I called him in and we drank hot tea until it
    was slopping about the dark shoreline
        of our skulls

Another time he came for milk and had a quiet fit
    on the kitchen floor. So I turned
him on his side. And every so often he stops me on
    the street and says "I don't owe you money,
        do I ?"

Since then he's got together with a battered woman
    from Galway. She is fierce and mild.
And he says they'll be married the first Saturday of
    Christmas month – bloodloss & wombsong –
        and to be sure to come

He still knocks for milk and money and for a talk
between friends. So we share hot tea,
two most landlocked of men left out on the ocean,
trawling away at the urban plankton that
drift around our skulls

A Song For Jean Harris

Born Leibowicz up Christian Street in 1924,
bombed out to Dorset, pregnant with the war,
her parents dead, her sister hit by the last
          V2 to drop on London

She worked in cafés but had a nervous burp.
Collected for kidney research in West End pubs,
she lifted bog rolls and jumbo dettols from
          the Ladies, always giggling

Her body was a building site dug by many men.
What they put up in her depths had hardened
glass edges and glistened with curt facades.
          Her kidneys always hurt

The Guinness Trust and Brady Street Dwellings.
Tea in the ABC with ageing Jews, her brothers and
spiteful sisters. If they called her a whore, I'm
          one too, writing this here

She died in the London from cancer of the guts
in great poverty and pain. Half a mile from her
we did not know. To her one son via a lawyer –
          40,000 put by on the way

I'm thinking of her five years past her death.
In Watney Market I often see her face – one of
the best I ever knew, she with the nervous burp
          and rope trick over all life

Fieldgate Streets

Windows of halved betel, of limes
and coriander and various chillies,
windows of crushed coffee bleating
in the deep blue of Aldgate night

And inside, slabs of frozen fish
Ganges and Padma fish and Bay fish
boul and fangus and rui and ilish fish
in the magical logic of cobalt night

Remember how it was during the day
the spaces between high tenements
hung with clothes of many colours
saris flapping the flags of dry air

And the man crazed with gambling
walks like an ice-hardened shirt
and shouts and spits on the pavement
all about the hostel stairs and closes

Zafar Uddin's won his court-case
Shahid still delivers each morning
David has gone at last to Cornwall
Carmel still dives the dry earth

I cock my head into the darkness
listen to the fish sucking hard air
watch harsh schizophrenic old men
and the blue Sylheti-English night

Praise Song For The Jewish Anarchists

Look at them lounging at the meadow's edge
Just where the suburb ends and forests begin,
Gentle anarchists carrying our deserted blood
Or holding hopes we had before we were born.
Kestrels nesting on the hospital's laundry roof
Green shoots sprung between the city's paving,
Cobbles of rain heard in the night's zinc light –
Or a fountain for those abandoned by language.
Through realities not recognised for being real,
Hawk-high as they fall away into azure space,
Through levels of dust and dazed – the Jewish
Anarchists of Hannibal Street and Cressy House.
Look at them ! Stands of oranges, pomegranates
Carp and apples and cheeses and plums and oil.
Set like matter's deft cohesion about to burst.
Such painting abandoned in a city's dead zone.
Such eyes held at the height of walking heads.
I'm looking at the old red anarchist tenements :
Slowly they rise up on the ebbs of night, then
Take their leave and go from the flooded seas.
The gentle intelligence of the urban anarchists
Are ships that pass by unnoticed far out to sea.
I am looking into the harsh daze of the future.
The air is still. Crates. Crushed fruit. Carp fins.
The eyes of cats. The eyes of drunken dancers.
Small half pieces of cheesecake with sultanas.
Nutmegs and layered almond and sweet burfi.
I light up twists of bidi and see another world.
Or the room is flooded with algebra and music.
Kammenitzer maggids sway on rotting chords.

And the sleepy anarchists are still sitting there
At the meadow edge a century in front of here.
In tense sadness for their world that is unreal
They are like phosphorescent fish in dense air.
As if all the roads of Whitechapel were rivers
And the fishmonger women simply had to furl
Their lines for carp or eel to wriggle onto stalls.
As if all the anarchists had to do was sleep or
Dream for the gala floats of language to arrive,
For the feast days of happiness to easily come,
For the banners of a commune to be unfurled,
For the clarinets of the sun to splash its music
      down all the days of our years.

House On The Highway

This house is like a vertigo, or like vertigo
    shoved backwards, so I
suppose it might separate from its neighbours
and rise at sudden speed into a strange orbit,
        this house

And although the stairs are not tall, I can
    sit on the top stair dreaming –
which is to say writing – and seem to plunge
into dark vestiges of the stairwell, although
        the stairs are not tall

Tiny flies rise in the ethers of this house as
    I have forgotten to
throw out old fruit for over twenty years now.
Come to my house, you will be well pleased
    by the delicate ethereal aromas

It is full of solid shadows, I cannot remember
    anything when I'm inside.
Cars passing by trawl tiny pellets of dusted air.
It is a real fiction and I can never believe in
    the existence of my house

Of course, it is full of books and mice make
    little nests after carefully
scanning lost poems. Moths are a problem too,
they refuse to speak. Come and read my books
    you will be lifted out of your self

And when it goes into its strange orbit, this
house, it is as if lacunae are
filled between my silences, and identical twin
khlebnikovs roam the irridescent taiga of my
desperate communal empire

Song For Mickie The Brickie

Mickie I met down Watney Street and he whistled
       me across. "How are
you" he said – and of course really meant "have you
a little to spare for some drink" – but could not
       bear to ask

We walked through the decayed market, a yellow-
       black sun gazed
down over Sainsbury's as I went to look for change.
Ten pound was hardly enough to get him through
       the dregs of that bitter day

We stood on the corner where for centuries people
       have stood. Many
worlds passed us by. When he had been in hospital
he'd taken his pills and been looked after and had
       not got worse

Now he's barely getting by. He walks out of the
       rooming house
in Bethnal Green when it gets too loud inside. His
scalp's flaking and he needs a reliable level and
       a small brickie's trowel

That woman's son's inside for good. That one's man
       is a chronic alcoholic.
This one's on her own and better for it. But how can
you know anyone's story when every day you walk
       by without stopping

Charlie Malone was a good friend. So was John Long.
        Now they're resting
in Tadman's Parlour – and first thing in the morning
Mickie'll go and say to them words that cannot be
                answered

Those are the best words, but they're hardest to bear.
        To me he says :
"Always – always – stop me – always – come across."
And what is the point of centuries of conversation if
        no-one's ever there to hear

A Song For Rocky

When first I noticed you, you were flicking
                    white slices of
bread from your wrist. They flew from one
platform to the other across the District Line
                    at Whitechapel

Food onto a slanted roof – for pigeon or gull.
                    Other times
you would be singing in the street or from
sacking spread at your feet you'd sell a few
                    shoelaces, a few shoes

You used to come into the Nelson, the Nelson
                    on Commercial Road – dirty and
drunk before you arrived. Once into the warm
you'd fall asleep, until the new landlord had
                    you thrown out

Students and nurses (wasn't I one of them ?)
                    walking into the empty pub
would finally challenge you to a game of pool,
not knowing what a cracked player you were
                    in the staggers of venom

You would clutch on the cue, eyeing it wrong,
                    before potting impossible
colours. The last time I saw you, you were sat
up Woods Buildings in a pool of cider bottles
                    singing after your sister

All singing fiction lies. I suppose that you are
dead now,
or in some other city – or in a city of the dead.
You have walked through the green zinc gates
with your besieged face

I will come and sit by while you tell me lying
stories. I will rise up and
walk through the market of melts and saltpetre
anxious to abort the sickness from the soul
of the city

Marginal Note In Time Of War

His name was not written
Hannah Arendt

Walter Benjamin took his own
life out of pure exhaustion, walking
into the mountains against love's gravity
up the scarp slope of his melting reason
to where he was abandoned by language.
Huge lethargies in the world glutted him
then stiff blood came, pulsed out in coils.
Who knows where he could have gone to
after that, except he couldn't go on, burst
by the butchered choice of angel history,
a tremendous shattering tossed across his
face, tiny maggots gobbling on sunlight,
fascisms in the honeys of his friendship.
His name unwritten, nowhere to be seen.
He who was the loveliest among people.
Why did no-one tell him when he lived ?
Nothing was left to hold him on the hill.
Angels could not put back insane reason.
Exhaustion killed him, more than terror,
more than despair, or a theology of dirt.
At the end – when the angel of history
called out his name to mock him – he
walked higher up into the blind frontier
and took his own life on a hillside that
looks over the sea : one of the loveliest
places on earth, as Hannah Arendt said,
	and like himself, halfway up
		and halfway down.

Travel Poem, Swallows ...

I shall not go to Siena and eat bread,
drink red Tuscan wine, walk with Franco
Fortini on the piazza that's like the sea,
meet up with Vladimir Holan on the road
        to San Gimignano

I shall not get to Rome or to Florence
or to the proletarian quarters of Milan. I
shall not go to the Alps where my grandfather was born, the razor's edge was
        stropped on the face of time

I shall not get to Venice by motorbike,
hank meat in Les Halles like Tudor Arghezi,
go to Athens by bus or East Iceland across
a pulsing sea. A dark sun is falling down
        an ash-stained sky

Blue swallows sink down the late day's
vortex and clouds buffet my ragged earth.
Somewhere each moment a man collapses
from hunger and women sift tiny rubbles
        from piles of rice

Hunger and poverty sieve the earth's blood.
Rich corpuscles remain, the blood's no good.
The hands of Giotto and Masaccio take up
our earth and give back colour to its ripe,
        undamaged substance

This earth is a cloth to cover our bodies.
Work or labour's sweat or singing madness.
And if I get to Rome or Florence or Siena
I shall still be here, stroking the earth's body
       and watching its colour rise

November Tree, Tower Hamlets

Another tree in the street has made me weep –
  its sharp and night-time shadow
    is not you.
You are a tramp who comes to my home asking
        for money,
you are my blinded neighbour, the young Sylheti
    lad kicked in the head,
you are the post-girl walking arm-in-arm with
      her Bangla friend,
you are my Muslim neighbour waving as I pass.
I look up in your branches : you are my mother.
I look up into you : you are my daughter and
        you are my son.
I look up : you are the commune that has never
      existed,
and the will to struggle and disperse a brutal dirt.
On the small plot of dogging green by the flats,
close to the highway in the zones of enterprise
      and indifference,
you are spread from core to air-pricked twig,
      rungs of
a ladder never broken that reaches to the burst
    heart of the sky,
little chamber where the voices come through of
    the tiny sisters who are always
      asking me questions.
You are an intricate cry raised against fascism in
    a crushed face,
raised against exhaustion that distorts the spirit.
But I wish neighbours would climb down from
    your branches to embrace,

I wish neighbours would walk into the rings of
                        your growth
and grow out to the vectors of your persistence.
I wish neighbours would love in their couples
                and love in their thousands,
and I look up into you and you are lovely and
                        you are intricate
and you are a tree, tall inverted lung near to
                my house that can breathe

Poem Of The Open Field

Not that there is a gate to be climbed
through in my lyric –
but what is a poem if not an opening
onto an open field

The white sutra climbed into the sun
o my burning crow,
a slabbed path descended to breath,
a gap to infinity

When magmas rose in circuits toward
the earth's crust,
red sulphurs burst on the steepled air,
already the open field was swallowing
our voices

And in the beautiful discourse of the
physicists, it was
the autistic poet who brought al-gebr
and music to the tongue

Giving to logic its lyric and its lemmas
and opening our eyes to
the most fertile and exacted images of
verbal disorder

Praise Poem For North Uist

Blood of my blood and you are on the hill
        of Eubhal and you go
brightflame are the waves among the islands
and the gannet sound that comes on the sea

And you are on the cold moors of Liernish
        and you go.
The straight line is the labyrinth memory
a steady unbearable decline from purging
          winter.

Love of my love and you are stood near
        the blue rooms of the sea
colour is multitude in the blizzard above
and in the bombs of air since that time

And you are on the wild coast of the Minches
        and you go,
great is the joy in the hearts of those people
and the anxiety that is pain in their limbs.

It was to there I went and to there I shall
        return if an image
takes me, if a blizzard takes my spirit, to
the eastern shore of a western island and
        the placid edge of the sea

Love of my love and you are stood on the little
        hill of Beinn na 'h-Airidh
and the sea goes to St. Kilda and Cuillin and Mull
and the sea rises through all the intricate stains
        of your heart

And you go among the small houses of Claddach
        strong is the kindness of those hurt people,
displacement of life and joblessness on those
        shores :
they gave you food – though you gave them none.

And you are sat in the back room of the black
        house,
damage and the smile of kindness on herself
and the burnt humour of his limping face ;
they gave you food – though you did not ask.

And you are on Grimsay at the big house calm
        in generosity, and the lady
of the house is like a young girl again with joy
at the coming of her daughters from America
        and Lochcarron

And you are at the shielings towards Locheport
        whoop of swan, heron and piled stone,
and their land is harsh and their townships
        cleared and their children gone.

And you are among the people of Grimsay, the
        bright roofs of their reticence
those who came back from the sea and those
        who did not come back.

And they are coming, postmen lobstermen men
        from the small shapes of the fields
and the peats, from the muds and the sands and
the quicksand, coming, coming, and which of
        them now will return ?

If I were to sing and if I were to put music
        to my song,
and to dance and drum the piled air, what
        praise would I not put on Uist

What praise and what harshness would I not
        put into my singing
measure of breath in the blizzard of these times
        but when have I ever finished a song !

Rising in a perfect curve upon the world's more
        perfect curve
in silent anger through the coma of this world
the mountain buried upright by the sea calls
        out to me.

My tongue moves in a dry mouth and I feel it
        swell.
It is the full sea come steering down beating
        song against generous hard cliff.

And if my mind were to go out to one man
        generous in his justice
then I would see the whole island with its
tongue exposed on the burnt edge of song.

I know how song arrives, that it comes with
          breath, that it is
a fire out on the waste, that the mouth is dry
and pain is laughter and I look for no excuse
          in my divided words.

And I am standing on the white cliff, I am
          on the other side of the mountain,
and the young cormorants slide into the lake,
sink and rise and sink in the exuberance of
          their wingbeat.

And I am on the other side of the mountain
          blood of my blood
there where no-one ever goes, a white sun only,
the lobster boat, the sheep man and the others
          I must not mention.

I am among the moor crests of that marvellous
          coast and I go
rock and timbers of the bandaged sun, and then
those friends who enter from the coma crests
          of their sleeps.

And I am there and there and there, as if
          from Tigharry to Bàgh Mòrag,
as if from the coast of Lochportain to the strand
          of Baleshare, North Uist was a city

Not a city of evil – but a haven – a city out
          on the wide spaces of the moor
in the wide generosities of those hearts. Stand
up now from the slow dark sessions of your
          sleep.

Stand at the fank, on the hill-slope and you can
see Carinish and the blight of Benbecula
(for the jobs it provided were not those that were
needed) you can see Heisker and Monach
and the whole spread of land and shattered sea

I am there as if Paible were full of yellow iris
amid the stooks of your happiness,
as if I could reach out and put hands on St. Kilda
as if the waves breaking white on white shores
were a sea rising about my heart.

Here I am far enough removed to reflect and
compose my mind,
to call up the single image of that wide earth,
and the broken thought of its dark shining
world.

Friends arrive, and they tread the abyss of
this silenced age.
The mountain wall is down and gone, the
shattered crown and raw pastures of the
slope.

I will not use irony in this poem, though it
copes and helps, that it won't be a
fatal implement,
that I won't be derelicted by a broken face.

I am stood on the lake, its steep and shattered
ice ; I am stood on the rocks and
a rucked moon creases the neat full sea. I am
stood on autumn shores to watch the world
go into darkness.

What mists and shattered land and plausible fog.
I shall not use irony to character those people.
A face speaks, a numb sun, a slow stain that
        moves across the sea.

I am stood on the rocks and out of the dense
        fogs of the landing stage
come sliding the boats of my hoard and my
        happiness.

And though I would have wished it to have been
        a community beneath that mountain,
beneath that mountain and over the whole of Uist
        from sea to air to sea and it wasn't

It was to the mountain I went, stepping out and
        in at the blue door – and
I would make this clear for those who wouldn't
        care to know :

It wasn't the loveliness of that land, hill and
        moor and inlet of the sea,
that took my mind and my mouth's spirit and
        made life's compulsion strong in me

It was not loveliness alone that took the ship
        of my song and my word horde
and spilt them easily, tilting snows across
        a superb sky.

I searched the belly, the face, the mountain.
        I asked with my eyes and heard the
        'Yes' 'Yes' 'Yes'
spring that follows the volcanic days of
        winter

Damage and hurt, the measure of faith, and
        edge of sight,
knowledge and speech put through my veins,
the smell of rain and generosity on a harmed
        face.

I have stood on the height of Berneray with
    the day coming over the sea.
I have taken the stone into my store : for
    what more can I ask ?

I have stood on the hill of Eubhal and have
        gone and been lifted,
and felt the laughter and yielding sobriety of
the ground. To what more can I lay stress
            and claim ?

And Uist has appeared to me like a boat, stern of
        Griminish from the prow of Eubhal,
and if it could drive us from pampered government
and if it could bring them to job-fulfilled shores –
    but when would that be likely.

I have stood on the slopes of the hill, the huge
        circle of its clear day,
the lucid algebra of its dialects, and sight that
    is the labyrinth of a straight line.

And from the slight peak of Beinn na 'h-Airidh
I will be seeing Benbecula no longer a crater
    but a set of kitchen gardens worked
        around Nunton.

I am standing on the wide sands of those shores
and I am racing and I am still and
I am there
and the mountain still animates this dark-shining
world.

And it is to there I shall return, if peace or an
ice blizzard take my spirit,
if a face speaks, a numb sun. And I will walk in
the door between the shoulders of that house.

I will walk in the door, blue chalk and poise
of the sun,
between the shoulders of the island, its rich turf
of time, ruined laughter and speech, and the
raw procession of those lives.

Climbing snowfalls and fences I will go at
the mountain's blade of bone.
Their sudden quiets and stillnesses, flame-birth
of compassion, the raw pastures of their bodies
and the fields.

And now they are coming – those who teach their
language and those who fish,
those who sheep or who shirk and those who wage
their lives against nothing, and those who return
and then go missing.

And I will not worry at my words' extravagance
(if they are cool houses spilled round with
bright air)
only whether my words are real, only whether
my rawness will become too inward.

And I give no excuse for the blind division of
    my words ; nor do they
need any. Nor you, those generous people, the
mountain, whose banners are the sea's and
        they are mine.

Spring 1976 or 1977, Whitechapel

Yosef Hayyim Brenner

I tried to write a novel about you – but could
not find my voice.
You were walking in it on the Mile End Waste
and the blue bag of language was slung across
your breast

I looked at you, looking right inside your face
but could not see
to where a pogrom of ships carried you across
the carp-dazed path as you went from Narod's
printshop to the post

I tried to envision the year but couldn't draw
out your blue.
When my mother was born near Soho Square
she was hardly three miles from where you
were

I think of the Jewish anarchists in Cressy House
and Hannibal Street.
They float in my mind – but do not stay. They
are like jellyfish I cannot hold : Rudolf Rocker
and the rest

The acid colour of daylight stings me but does
not sting my memory.
I crave a touch of calm hands that might unmake
our century and rewrite time as we would have
it be

What is this sulphur of red sunlight, words and
their contagions ?
I think of the Italian anarchists of Clerkenwell,
the cafés in Frith Street, blond faces in nitrogen,
clarinets of the sun

I look across at the London Hospital that's newly
dressed in scaffolding
and I adjust the blue bag across my breast, feel
the wet fish and its ginger shift inside my old
anarchic cave

What is this sulphur of red sunlight ? This quest,
my breathless brother,
for the oxygens of our daily breath, this struggle
to avoid torture ? I wait. I wait. I wait. Singing
on a carp-dazed street

And at last I see you walking in a peaceful rage
under the blind sun.
Your face beneath all that weight of time is lit up
as you climb the ladder through the red sulphurs
of the sky

What 31 Children Said About Dreams

And Paul said
> everywhere I walk in my dreams only white shines
> in a circle all around me and I am in a boat
> and I am in a different world

and Sadia said
> dreams are like water flowing, dreams are like
> flowing water, with bubbles and bands,
> with greens & with creams

and Carly said
> there are neither laws nor limits in dreams and in
> dreams anything can happen, and my dreams
> are luminous turquoise

and Daniel said
> dreaming is like thinking and thinking is like dreaming
> and the pictures in your mind they are moving and
> they are still, and the colours in your dreams
> are all blurry

and Lauren said
> she wasn't sure about dreams, but then she painted
> a perfect dream, the underwater of it
> all cream air and the surface full
> of float and separating parts

and Olando said
> dreams are stripy (like when you draw on top of
> a piece of wood) and dreams are like when
> your dad parks his car in a strange
> unusual place

and My Van said

> there was a big circle of magic after we came
> back from the music room and the room
> of dreams, and My Van said many
> other things as well

and David said

> you relax, you go to sleep in your mind, you go to
> another world, you concentrate on something
> else and it comes to you far away in the
> wilderness and the wind makes
> circles of whistling

and Emma said

> the moons and the suns are circles and God's love goes
> round and round and never ends, and dreams are
> somewhere else, in music maybe

and Charley said

> things happen in dreams very suddenly and in
> there everyone is in a magic circle and
> everyone is a magic circle and that
> is why

and Karris said

> it was a dream spell, it was an eye dream, it was
> a cover round the sun, it was a pirate hat,
> it was a numb leg in my sleep

and Charlotte said

> it was like gliding down the rainbow, it was a
> magic carpet to go on, and you can put it
> in a frame like a picture,
> your dream

and Henry made
           a dream boat out of blue folds and sailed away
              on it (but he came back and told us) and
              a dream is like a sunflower and this
                    is just a dream

and Aimee said
           its a napkin, its a handkerchief, yeah, he's sailed
              away, and when she slipped under the table
              we all thought she'd startled an action,
                    she'd started on a dream

and Billy said
           there was a boy on his estate, there were racing
              pigeons on his estate, there was a monster
              on his estate, yeah, and he could tell
                    us a dream for sure

and Kelly said
           goblins pop out with your sick and dreams are
              magic because they happen real quick
              and dreams are like tambourines
                    and the air's wavey lines

and Melanie said
           the story of Bluebeard's Castle without quite knowing
              who Bluebeard was, and she said the only place
                 something can be something else is
                    in a dream (a garden be a
                    moon, for instance)

and Babs said

> when people dream it feels like its really happening
> and then sometimes it really does and sometimes
> it doesn't, and Babs is a pastmaster
> of what happens, he sure is

and Katie said

> its a bandanna, its got decorations, I think its the
> sun and we all looked out of the window
> and suddenly we noticed
> it was trying to snow

and Ted said

> when I'm in bed I have a dream and I see red (or so
> it seems), if I see blue I know its true, but I
> don't see blue (do you see blue ?)

and Justine said

> there was a big yellow bird, big as a table, and it
> stretched its wings and it called me bad and
> it bit me, but I know that bird was bad,
> that big yellow bird in my dream,
> and not me

and Marvin said

> I think it was a butterfly and then it was a sunflower,
> then it was a flower garden and then it was a
> cloth for shadow puppets (now you see
> nothing, now you see every-
> thing, now you see)

and Kieran said
in sleepwalking your imagination steers you in
your dream and he said in his dreams he
hears English and Chinese and Irish
and Jamaican and Antiguan

and Chelsea said
in my dream there was a plane in blue skies and it
made me very happy and the birds looked like
they were singing and the sky was
very deep, like the sea

and Rachel said
she sometimes had a hidden rope behind her
back and she could disappear up it into
the nice blue sky, into the warm
just so we couldn't see her

and Khaled kept
his words to himself and he drew his words in exact
and detailed images and his imagination was
precise and he remembered everything
with perfect clarity

and Dominique said
words come out of my mouth and they become lines
and they become circles and they become flowers
and they become butterflies and they become
lily-pads and they become dreams
and they ...

and Marie said

        you sneeze, you cough, you hiccup, you speak,
        you stop – and the fish swim round in your
        dream and boats float on a blue
        crystal sea

and Callum said

        when you say 'hello' to the night, you dream and
        its like a hundred years go by very fast
        and when you wake all you can
        remember are fizzy colours

and Janine said

        my dreams are in my head and in my eyes and in
        my bed and the dancer hid under the table
        and the singer looked there for the
        magic word

and Jamie said

        it's a moon, it's a sun, it's a bell, it's a cloth, it's
        a window, it's a scarf, and it comes out of
        your head, your dream, and it comes
        and it comes without words and
        without end

December 1997 after workshops with children

A Typeface For Amanda

Your body smelled of type and menstruation,
of the strong evoked blocks of print made flesh
and the serene unpassive towers of your blood.
And your body smelled of apple and cut apricot
of fresh cloths soaked in air that wrapped bread.
You were like a young Muslim at fasting prayer.
And your body smelled of darkness with traffic
of wall posters slapped onto hoarding with spit
of meals eaten with lost money in student cafés
of tube trains squealing out of stations like pigs.
Your body smelled of the shuttle of sweat work
machine and sweat and ache of singing labour
of money sent each month to homeland villages.
Your body smelled of calm and revolving cogs.
Of all these your body had the undoubted glow,
not just one part of your body, but the whole of
you, each cell and breath space, every corpuscle.
Just a few times we slept close to each other and
it was good, it made our breathing become calm,
it made what is beautiful glow light on our skins.
We were without the careless hates that destroy,
destroying not just two lives, but all living, with
cynicisms that blunt loves down to beaten grief.
We were as dear animals asleep with each other.
Your body smelled of typeface and menstruation.
When the word became flesh what was beautiful
in our human spirits rose to your skin's surface
        and stayed there and quietly glowed

A Song For Alieu Sadankay

Big Al! You've been on your holiday. How many
        months of forced vacation,
how many weekends of tight reprieve did you have ?
We will meet again in Maytime to enjoy the richer
        fictions of the summer sun.

Nothing has changed in Shadwell or in Watney,
        the Thomas Neale is still
that filled aquarium from where we drinking fish
watch the moving picture of the market daze as
        we cross the bridge of dreams.

Big Jennie still walks with her kids up that street
        slow with the god of speed.
Railed arches shake with the sweats of withdrawal.
The trains are all gone. You know what I mean,
        I know that you do.

Your father – a great tailor of the world – sewed
        the seamless garment in Whitechapel.
He who moved between Mayo and Morocco like
a vessel trading in leather and music, leaving a
        few threads for your self.

We all of us shake with the sweat of making love
        or from being locked in.
Golden meadows stretch before our eyes : sight is
the trick our mothers taught us to get us through
        and mothers are strong.

We will meet again in Shadwell in the summer sun
and the market of our mid-days.
With juice or beer – Alieu Sadankay – we'll erase
the white fear in your face, the chalk marks of all
that you were forced to.

Moorland With Fire And Snow

All the colours of snow imminent in the sky
    that is coming,
black and brown obelisks in a dance of light
birds whorling white beaks in front of an
    unshattered curtain,
gulls whose backs become white as they spin
    against the breaking air,
green flecks that are owl flight in front of
    the storm,
fire when the prayer wheels burn in cartons
    of raw light,
crimson flame when mountain tenements go
    staggering on singed air.
This is language that is forming in my throat
revolt of burst energies from the skies of my
    silence,
snows that tossed dead gulls across the moor,
in the perfect circle of dawn they are strewn
    about the shorelines,
in the exact geometries of morning they are
    bruising my veins.
Remember the tortures and the poetry, and
    the fertile crests of the white-out,
the horses of laughter, the nostrils that foam,
the sermons on barbarism, and the struggle
    against butchered choice.
This is language that is forming from a clot
    in my throat,
a torch of fire out on the wasteland, a tent of
    heat beneath the mountain,

a little drinking fountain for those abandoned
by language,
a spray of paint on democracy wall, democracy
wall that does not exist.
Moorland with snow and fire : a far-off burnt
headland has stood up in my blood – it is
trickling its crystals down the garnet
air.

Vision Of My Life In The Year 2040

I will be talking with my mother close to my death
I will be wrapped in a blue plaid cloth and I will be
          sitting at the edge of the sea
those bodies will be burning out on land's dark spit
that bicycle will come down the incline all of its own
I will hear the train arriving over the slope and bells
          of cows in the fermenting town.
This will be well on in the next century and I will be
          talking to my mother as I wait

Mountains like broken teeth will be glistening across
          the placid sea
horses will be ridden over the island's white pastures
they will eat sea-pinks and buttercups and go down
          tilted shores for cochineal of weed
townships will be repeopled, lost languages regained.
Schist rubbles accommodate the straggle of mourners
as I sit out the white war of winter rage and drift on
          the bridge of dreams

At the frontier of the mountain town my twin uncles
          will die of german measles
thirty years before I am born, and a cart carrying my
mother's mother will pull into the bomb-pocked town.
My father will duck under the belly of a running horse
          rivers will join and be parted again
wooden bridges be trampled in a rut of vodka apples
I will be talking with my mother, close to the stretto
          of final exhaustion

Whatever has happened with me and my friends or in
the rotting gut of community,
shadows passed across a face, memory's blade of bone,
the final stretto made between language and silence is
set in a vision of clotted sanity that flickers on my eye
and time is flaking away, o
dear and tender body, o ebbing breath, and syllables
will collide to form a poem and birds will fall out of
the unprophesied air

Therefore, as I look from the next century back to this
through the shark-tooth visioned sea,
through veils of rain that run across the distant waters
I will see a sorghum cart turn in at mountain pastures
vagrants will pour from it, my self and my grandfather
among the refugees of time.
And the frontier of the mountain town will give way to
spits of black schist and far-off maritime lights entice
me back to or out from life's dream.

A Very Little Light

Uma pequenina luz
Jorge de Sena

Simply for the breath of staying alive
  I should talk to you,
simply to pass some words across a table
   as bread or oil,
and not have them die in me. Or
      die in you.
    And as I
measure by measure slowly toss the crisp
herbs of speech over towards your face,
a very little light will come into my eyes,
   a very little light
will glow out at you and enter your eyes
and will be returned to me and calm our
   mouths against duplicity.
And when all the bitter fratricides are
   piled up about us
this little light, this tiny flame out on the
    waste patch,
this wind-shaped tent that is your eye
   with its slow torch,
this flickered heart with its ventricles
    that beat and pump,
will provoke in us a bonfire and the will
    to live,
and even from the embers there will glow
   a little light, a very little
   shining light,
as we pass some words across the table,
   simply for the breath of
    staying alive.

Alexander MacDonald

I have never been in Arisaig where you
    live in an unknown grave, and
those who remain are beneath the bright
    roofs of their reticence

Whether the sea is that dark swirling
    that sobs in our hearts,
whether it will become the white quiet
to our rioting, I cannot reject what
    life or sea may bring

The words of your sea-stained poem rise
    but evade my passionate mind. I
can only believe the endurance of lives
    or else the failures to endure

Is that breath the sea, ebbing and
    sobbing from its neap ?
Is that the sea that took away families
    flickering there on your tongue ?

From where I look, telescoping you
    from island or city, I can
see only poisons arrayed in odd tubes,
the masks of the world we are made to
    look through

And as I look now towards Arisaig and see
    the risk and rift of it, I know
it will break us open, spines ripped out, or
ease from our curtailed mouths a sea-tide
    of needed speech

Mark Wickham In Whitechapel

I am sitting in the Wimpy Bar and it is just
              as if it were a year ago :
Mark Wickham is sitting in the empty chair
and he is eating a plate piled high with fish
              and chips

And sauce and salad – and everything else.
He is asking the waitress to take the skin off
            from his fish, then he is asking
her to take the batter off. Then he is asking
              for a cloth

And for a glass of water from her. Then if she
            will let him have a kiss.
These are not the usual duties in a Wimpy Bar.
And I am wondering does she yet realise what
              the matter is.

He is telling me that his lovely friend is very
            ill : and he is positive she
will not live. And because he needs to he will
want to kiss her somewhere on a nearby face
            as he leaves the Wimpy Bar.

I met him on the Mile End Waste – that great
            mad market of the
world – and knew by the absence of his yellow
bike and the grey fleck in the pain of his eye
            that he needed to talk

He mentioned Richard. He talked about Carmel
     and the lovely bus-driver Cleo.
And Ferenc – that Hungarian survivor – and John.
He who lived in Adelina's Grove down the ghost
     days of his life

He talked of everything in that day-long hour,
     a semiotics for the cinema,
grain and constitution, sugars in his cups of tea,
skirting round or holding down, then plummet-
     lining on his fear

I missed his funeral – was not and yet was sure
     that he had died.
And write these words in memory of an ordinary
maddened man, and the compulsive sadnesses
     he had to leave behind.

Song For My Daughter

After you had been on this earth seven days
            you took your leave of it.
We knew you were dying only on the seventh day
and your mother held you in her arms and sang
            the lullaby of your breath.

You were born in one hospital and died in another
            with an ambulance drive between.
That was the only journey you made on this earth
other than the voyages inside your mother's womb
            and I was near to you all that time.

One ride in traffic through the crushed ventricle
            of London streets.
But what could you have known of any of that ? I
who registered your birth and death in one go
            do not know what you know yet.

Your mother sang you a Hindi lullaby as you went,
            o little lovely body of the ebbing
breath, she held you in her arms. Both of us were near
you, but could not go with you, nor could we mend
            the bruised aorta of your heart.

Neither aura nor language were given you, nor
            that we should recover the past.
Neither pain nor laughter nor the singing madness.
You who were born not to be, in the heart of
            this world.

My Mother, Her Tongue

When you died I was not with you. The struggle
          I saw on your mouth,
was it the struggle to accept or to reject ? Did calm
perturb you on the raw pastures of the level
          slope ?

You who lived fifty years in the same house,
          what happened when you passed
from there into the simple language of silence ?
What mother tongue dialect rose in your throat
          before being reeled back.

Did you remember in those last hours the silent
          film of your childhood,
did the dialects of reality crystallise in your voice,
each image of war and peace fading from a sky
          of crushed mango ?

When you died I was not with you, I had left you
          two days before,
thinking you would be here for three years, more,
that the red mountain of blood would not explode
          or death struggle rise to your mouth

Now your body is gone, your discourse is gone,
          your spirit is departed.
I strain to call back your voice and talk from my
lungs, but somewhere I know colliding waters
          have dissolved the mother tongue.

V.

Journey Across Breath

Mountain Language

Grandfather look. At the soldiers wading
through that high snow. Up to the calves
of their snowboots. Up to the Pian d'
Adamello and the white winter passes
and the black crags that jut up to the sky.
Look, do you see ? Do you see them ?
Look how fast they are moving through
the century, how slowly they are moving
through the snow ! Look how the archive
of the burning air is sifting under their
boots. Can you feel it ? Can you feel
anymore ? Can you feel the mountain and
the snows and the bones and the metal
and the skin dissolving into spans of
brown time ? Can you feel now that you
are no longer dead ? Can you sense the
melted mess of your brothers ? How long
will this immensity of space and the
gristle of our languages last ? I am sorry.
Please forgive me, I cannot contain now
what I am wanting to say. Across the
snows hundreds of soldiers in single file
move, the film of them winding out across
blurred edges centred on a dazzling
white. The sun off the snow fields in their
eyes is blinding their sight. Memories
from a mother's childhood. Furls of
barbed wire and bursts of shell, pieces of
heavy gun pulled from the passes by dogs
and donkeys and the valley floor below,
tunnels bullied through wads of ice, creak

and riposte of glacier, trace of a hunter
from five thousand years ago, bodies held
up in crevasses for the dead journey of a
lifetime, bone and leather held up in slow
moraines. So many soldiers beaten by
maps, swallowed in the little fratricides of
brown time or by murders impossible to
detect or improve upon or even define.
Masks and toggles, the science of helmets
and goodbyes, the snowshoes of sentinels,
boots with animal skins turned inward,
gear of hair and pelt, cervices of lice and
white dust, soldiers with ski-sticks
splayed out on the snow, machine-guns
exploding in the rifugios, trench lines
near the ski huts, white war of first winter
ascents, white war coiling in the heart of
Europa. Heart bursting with blood,
crushed ventricle, exhausted aorta,
calcified passages, decayed vessel, lung
with the hair grown inward, Europe of
loves and of hatreds, Europe of
stupidities, Europe of an insane grasping
after premature sanities. Haemorrhage of
the heart, dear body, dear body, dear and
breathing body. Grandfather look at the
soldiers moving through the snows of
your memory, they are swallowed by
faded maps and melted in yellow
geographies or foetid puddles. Mountain,
bone, face, tongue, language, culture,
heart melted into old water. Cold and
greasy soup. Metallic taste. Tell me how
you felt in the capital of a far-off country

hearing this shrapnel of news, these word-
shreds, never really knowing, catching
echoes of the exploding geographies and
then that other haemorrhage readying
itself to burst with immaculate and white
irony inside your head. And your cousin
Bortolo out in the January blizzard,
dieing of peritonitis the year after the war
was over, no doctor able to make it across
the snow-meadows, or the snows of time,
to arrest the irruption of his appendix.
Forgive me, nonno, I cannot properly put
into words that which I meant to say.

* * *

To get up at six in the morning. To put
your head out at the skylight and look at
the mountain before dawn. To see the
infinite outline of a straight line. To see
the blue of day before it has become blue.
To see where stalks of lightning were
planted in the air above the rooves. Black
coffee and dry bread. The main street and
then its curve. A second strong coffee in
the bus station café. The room you slept
in when you first came to the town. The
plunging river that dances down the
moon. The zig up past Fulvia's old school.
And out onto the mule path that leads to
Villa d'Alegno. The grass frozen, the
earth in small ruts. The sun is starting to

rise somewhere far down the valley. The slight curdle in the milk of the air. Your footfall on secure ice. Glass needles on the edges of tilth. Little un-slipways out onto the strips of meadow. The words that fall from your tongue to your fingers. The shoulder scarf that is tied round your waist under a coat. The frozen path rising slightly all the way to Villa and the higher *baite*. The edge of the mountains high on the other side of the valley. DNA of mediaeval contadini in the slivers of rose bushes and of contrabandi in the sluice holes of wall. Route taken by pack-animals through the centuries. Taken now by you in your ludic folly. Just before Villa d'Alegno instead of continuing into the village – which is another story, its wall paintings, its stone barns, its partisans – you leave the path and steeply climb a meadow. Frozen ruts, frozen grass to hang on to. And the sun a white circle rising behind your back painting its light across the hoar field. Just where you reach a higher path – since this whole hillside is a sonata of crossing paths – just at the meadow's edge, a crocus with its yellow face looks right into yours and you greet each other and silently weep. The higher path leads you gradually into the snow. Through thick woods. Past mountain houses where dogs bay at your footfall. Where wood piles are alphabets you can just decipher. Snow drifts more thickly over the path and you realise you have come too high. Down through the thinning trees as best you can. Down toward distant cow-bells. Down there a mist follows the plunging river and curls about the houses. You and the sun are above it. Finally you get to the *baita*. Wreiths of snow still banked in its shadow. Off with your scarves and coat and boots. You sit in the warm sun and find that you melt into the silence. Giacomo in his spirit still here if he's still anywhere. *Ca de Jac*. Your mother is sitting up on the wooden balcony in the August sun in the last year of her life. Fulvia is feeding the dog Bobo at the same time as she is just getting up in Brescia. You take out a card and write it to her. You say "the postman managed to get this far on 24th February". And you put it in a crack of the sloped door out of the winds to come. Weeks later her uncle Annibale will find it and tell her. Then you walk down past Giovanni's empty *baita*. Past the places of wild strawberries. The zig and zag of the path down to Precasaglio. Past the house that belonged to your grandfather until the '39 war. Past the graveyard in the mountains and the road-fork at Zoanno. The river that goes plunging through the town. Mid-way through the morning. Everyone is up. Strong black. Latte. Shared lunch. In two hours you'll leave for Brescia and the

airport at M ... As for the *baita*, isn't that
the only way to get back to where you
need to be : the long way round, the arc
away from where you are going, in order
to get there. The unlogic that gives
richness to journey. That lets you pass
through the present to the past and back
from the past to your future. That allows
the white sun to rise behind you and call
the yellow crocus of winter to its
motionless dance.

* * *

January 3 : Rifugio Bozzi. You should not
be here. It should not be possible to walk
this high at this time. Two thousand four
hundred and seventy five metres. But
nonetheless here you are. With Salvatore
Ferrari, who is called Satana. Sharing his
salami and cheese and wine. Taking a
gulp of grappa against the coldening of
the air. Thick shirt. Worn face. You met
up here. Both of you surprised. You in the
staggers of snow ecstasy. He with the
quotidian possibility of some work.
Stretched lamb's wool of a sky. Thin air
combed and carded where your eyesight
tries to go. With grappa and coffee you
climb up the drifts to the point of the pass
and look down the wide and stark valley
of the other side. Earlier in the day you'd

taken the bus to Pezzo and then walked
up the valley to Case di Viso. Because it
was possible and, more important, a
lovely thing to do. Among the winter-shut
houses and small marker graves of the
partisans suddenly it seemed plausible to
walk on higher. A few patches of snow.
That was all. Then tyre marks. Some
words written in the air. Looking up at
the snow level. Realising how high it was.
And then starting to climb. The last three
hundred metres wading through waist-
high snow. Knowing that the rifugio was
just over the slight ridge : where the
down-slope would begin and not right in
the hollow. Being pulled upward by the
blind blue sky. Making for the arc of
ridge. Knowing where the rifugio was and
getting there as if to a home, but not
expecting its door to be open. Wondering
who had driven the jeep up the zig-zag
track but not expecting its driver to be
here. Then here it is. The home reached
when it should not have been possible.
When it should have been a house inside
its own igloo, in its own snow-cave of
hibernation. Astonishment on Salvatore's
face. This man who doesn't speak much
Italian ! Simple sharing of food and
drink. Isn't this how language forms ?
Though this was achieved in much silence ?
A few words. The sky and its colour.
January and its mystery. Film stills
separating themselves out and spilling

over. In one of them a shepherd gathering
in his sheep. In another partisans coming
down off a mountain. In another a small
avalanche about to crush a ledge and its
path. And then finally, soldiers inching
their way across a snow field.
The insanity of a moment in time. The
impossibility of a moment out of it.
Salvatore looks up, hands me a glass of
coffee. The warmth of it with its finger of
grappa. The sun about to start on its fall.
The key in the lock. The steep descent
straight down to the jeep. The ice drive
down the zagging track. The white graves
of the partisans. The winter-tight cluster
of houses. The road where in the summer
adders would be run flat. This strange
sense of flowering ahead in winter. Back
into Pezzo without stopping this time. The
darkness that is falling as we get into
Ponte. A quotidian coffee in the hotel's
backroom. The dark calm of the
basement kitchen. Domenica thinking of
her childhood. And my grandfather : why
had he left this valley ? But why did I
think he ever had an alternative, driven
as he was through brown time.

* * *

One lunchtime, or late in the morning,
when Giacomo had gone early into the

dining-room in something of a bad mood, I went and sat with him – out of sympathy really and because I wanted to be with him when he was so sad and angry. We had soup and then some salami and bread and we spoke little but were glad of each other's company. Wilma brought the food in – being in the hotel we could not go and fetch it ourselves – and Silvana looked round the door to see how things were. As we were taking some last pieces of bread Giacomo's brother Giuseppe arrived and sat with us. A conversation immediately sprang up between the two of them. As if their last conversation had simply been interrupted by the passage of time since they were last together. As if what they had been saying to each other had lasted a whole lifetime. These two men nearing seventy who had been in discourse since before they could remember. These two who had exchanged words across a table or by the side of a road or on a sheep path in the mountains or at one or another *baite* for near on three quarters of a century. Does time matter in such portions or such bundles ? How long does it take to start a conversation ? Will it be finished after seventy years ? And what does it take to end it ? They talked, eating along the way almost as an aside, bread and cheese and wine. I could not follow them exactly as they used the dialect of Precasaglio for the most part and occasional words from the vocabulary of local shepherds. They talked about old pastures and stands of fir trees that one or the other of them had lease or ownership over. They talked about the snowfalls of the past winter and some small avalanches and the high November winds that had torn down stanches of trees. They mentioned how long it was since anyone had died in the valley in an avalanche and remembered the terrible deaths of 1929 when they'd been very young. A lot left unsaid. The war and the partisans skirted by or told with a silence. I stayed at the table with them as they wanted and was able to understand at least this much. Nothing was said of Giuseppe's health but clearly he was not well. I stayed at the table with them while all the other tables emptied. I heard the dialect that my mother had understood, the dialect of my grandfather. I saw language forming in front of me, felt it, was palpable with it, let it into my writing hand and my pulse. The science of goodbyes and the difficult crafts of silence. A little miracle of tongues overcame the mesmerised air and then the electric tremor settled. How could we have known that within one year Giacomo would no longer be alive, knocked down by the cancer that his brother was so clearly suffering. How could we have known that Giuseppe

would have survived him, clinging on in
bleached silence through his own pain.
What has happened to their words that
were left hanging all about the villages
and valley, for words do not disappear
but carry on singing in the air. In the
grasses, in the wild mushrooms, in the
tree branches, in the snows of the village
and the dust of the town and in the torn
memories of our depleted but never
melancholic selves.

* * *

The day of Giacomo's funeral white light
splashed all down the valley and poured
over the church spilling in through the
high windows. Giacomo who had never
really believed in a benign god, and who
had nothing but scorn and hatred for one
that was not benign. But the priest spoke
of him with generosity, as a human being
who had lived seventy honest years in the
town and its villages, struggling not only
for his life, but for others' too. Red and
blue bands of light came through the
stained windows and the church packed
with friends of that solitary man. His
distraught daughters – who after all had
not known him in his early years – were
amazed that so many had turned out at
his death. That so many had stopped off

their lives for a few moments to wait for
his. Or said words of respect and
struggled warmth to Domenica and
themselves outside the church. And out in
the thin white air there were so many as
well. The steep rise up to the steps was
difficult to pass through and many could
not get in at all. The opened arms of the
'god be with you' and then what the
priest knew he had to say : for he had
talked often enough to Giacomo over the
years, even if hardly ever in church. After
the requiem mass the cortege started out
for Precasaglio, taking the road over the
turbulent river, ascending the rise of slats,
under the bridge of the house, out on the
flat yards past Ferrari's wood-yard,
taking the zig and the zag to the level of
Zoanno, following in reverse the journey
Giacomo had taken so often on foot, to
the graveyard of the mountains and the
niche in the wall that now was his and
where his photograph would be placed
when this last curve was done. Further
into Precasaglio the church where
Sebastiano's altar rail was carved. Past
the plunge down the ravine's slope
to the torrent below. By now
it was raining a cool trickle, or
hardly raining : enough to make the tent
posts damp. Enough to wet the earth of
the graveyard. Enough to let the adders
raise their may-time heads. Enough to
send you up to the *baite* for when it might

stop. That was the miracle of the day : after such a life of silences and quiet, of animated talk only, or so it had seemed, with his brothers and a very few friends, after a temporary history of averted faces, suddenly so many unsuspected tributes and generous words for the dead man and the life he had lead. So much remains hidden to the closest child. Herding on the other side of Gavia in early summers and journeys with the sheep all the way down to Cremona. Days with the partisans and then the cattle truck across the Brenner, the unspoken incarcerations for two years. The return after the war, marriage, family, summer labours, winter stock, all the time his pastoral economy being straitened out of his life. Remembering outside memory who had said and who had not said, who had done and who had not done, and who had denied doing. Pulling him into the last decade of the century. Pulling him to where memory fails. All that morning white light was splashed through the valley as if poured from his mother's jug, and then about noon a slight and warm drizzle settled in on the levels of words and meadow fruit.

* * *

Fulvia's sister runs the hotel now. She
does well enough. It is hard work for
them all, Mariangela, Domenica and Silvi
too. It's not what they might have chosen,
it's what they've had the courage,
to do. Economic necessity can also be a
prison-house. It is the Albergo Pineta in
the fork of the road that runs past the
car-park that used to be the square where
the market was held in the years after the
war. The market still does put itself down
there every Wednesday, trousers and
cheeses, boots and bacons, winter coats
and salamis, bed-sheets and shoe-laces,
gloves and underwear, and even
some tables of good books, a bookshop that
travels by van from place to place. Until
1960 or so the square was on the edge of
the town : now it has been swallowed up
and its geography extended by apartment
blocks and flats of the milanesi and
hotels. Albergo Pineta is one of these. The
first time I went there, in 1979 I suppose,
the old kitchen was still used by my
cousin's family and I even now find it
difficult to stand in the wide airy vestibule
where once Giacomo had made and
scooped out huge pats of polenta for the
stew, where Silvana once had frothed
milk puddings to a whisked cocoon and
any sister's child who happened by would
be called in to sit down and eat. Not that I
am mis-remembering a golden time.
Rather I am just trying to understand

how we've all got here to where we are
now and what might have happened in
the interim. For years there was a cherry
tree just in front of the hotel in the fork of
its garden and in summer we sat in its
shade and talked over tiny cups of coffee.
Coffee in these mountains is the best :
either black and dense, or in bowls
frothed with hot milk. Exactly where we
were, men fifty years before had walked
by with big lambs in their arms and sheep
crowded in behind. Shepherds on their
walk to Cremona eight days away.
Breaths that can be measured at the pace
of walking take their time to die down :
but something would happen after each
war, something that can barely be
articulated but that meant change,
something both sudden and gradual, seen
in half-glances and near neighbours not
talking to each other for years, eyes
averted, spans of memory and wilful
forgetfulness. White light is poured across
the valley as from a jug and the sun
climbs the morning sky. In a far-off *baita*
someone is washing mushrooms for
risotto and the mushrooms have come out
of the woods. An adder is biting into a
tiny and tart strawberry before slithering
out onto the hot road to be flattened
under a passing wheel. Mariangela is
maybe halfway through her married life,
Luigi comes from the village of Saviore
way down above Cevo. With two

daughters growing towards school who still think that English must be some dialect of Italian. She stands a minute contemplating her day. Then gets on with it, calls out to one of the hotel-maids, puts her head in at the kitchen to catch the eye of the chef, checks out in the same moment the risotto and the veal, nods a message to Silvana that says a whole morning without the need for words, remembers in time both about Anna's shoes and Giulia's books. She does well enough. All of them do. It is hard work for them all. It is not what she might have chosen, but it is what she has. She carries it all with dignity and a mild harshness that is steeped in ordinary time. A little like my mother when she was living through her busy years.

* * *

On that day of withered tongues we set out to go to Edolo in a car, my cousin Fulvia driving like a herded witch on the wrong side of the road, crowning bends on laughter. Not that she was a bad driver. On the other side of the valley time was one month behind and we went down through Temù and Stadolina, Vezza d'Oglio and Incudine. Five kilometres short of Edolo we turned off

up the hill to the village of Monno where
the folk group '*di Munnu*' lived. We sat in
the back kitchen of Pierin's shop while he
showed us various instruments and
books. It was quiet there in that village in
the middle of summer, quieter than it had
been for centuries. As quiet as if Paul and
Benjamin's angel of history had brushed
its wing along the valley's side missing all
contact with this cluster of houses and
church. Later we drove higher up the
road towards Passo Mortirolo until the
car caught itself in a slow semicircle and,
blocking the path of a cart coming down
from the heights, we completed our circle
and came back down by ourselves. It was
early afternoon by the time we got as far
as Edolo. In the bookshop, crammed and
old with all sorts, we bought a few
children's colouring books
and an old copy of Beppe Fenoglio's '*La
malora*' and Gadda's '*Diario di guerra e
di prigionia*'. Plus a book by the dialect
poet from the township of Vione, Dino
Marino Tognali. Then in the warmth we
went to the café Vasko Mora and sat
outside, the three of us, with iced coffees
and lemon juices, in the sun under the
buzz of time. On the corner where the
through road takes one bend before
taking another under the stone arch that
bridges the river and out of Edolo along
the Frigidolfo back towards Ponte. Years
passed us by, years going backwards

down a warm tunnel brown and blanched
with light. Traffic got thinner and the air
too thinned out a little. And suddenly as it
got toward evening a cart came past, a
wooden cart pulled by a horse. And my
mother was in the back of the cart though
she had been dead three years and she
was a young girl just entering her teenage
years. I watched her go past me seventy
years before where we were – unable to
leap up and call out – sat outside in the
sun. A war had just ended and she was
travelling to her father's village on the
frontline from London in the year of the
great and terrible 'flu epidemic. I saw her
going past, the angle and edges of her face
set fast in the air just as I knew her, the
tilt of her neck just as she was in the chair
and patience of her old age. I saw who she
was as she passed us by on the way to her
town pocked with bomb blasts. She went
with the cart under the bridge and
plunged upwards with the reversed river
along the warmed side of the valley out of
my sight. Then slowly, slowly the brown
tunnel melted us back into the light of the
late afternoon where we were in the
turning year and we got up, the three of
us, and drove our way calmly back to the
Pineta in Ponte, finding that tourist
town's walls no longer pock-marked with
bomb blasts and shrapnel from
the ancient war.

* * *

Grandfather, there was once a man who
became a shepherd. He went up to
Motta Varuna in early June, to the
mountain slopes above Cadera and the
curling railway and the paths over above
Somdos and he stayed over through to the
snows of late October. He stayed there
and he made cheese and he thought the
skin of the flanks of the cows was sleek
and he saw the udders of the cows as taps
that could be turned off or on. Cheese and
bread, curds and rice and whatever he
could get hold of. Twenty kilos of
mountain cheese and the crisp herbs of
speech talking there to the udders in cow
dialect, to the cows in mountain language.
Was it good in the mountains where
kidneys of rock were springs beneath the
skin. Where livers of the pasture were fed
on green glacier water. Where the
pancreases of the cows were sluiced on
aerial sugars. Where the sun hung in
balance fell suddenly over the crests of
the stone-wall. Cheese and rice and
whatever he could get hold of. He walked
on the slopes above Motta Varuna and
the soles of his feet made small paths
through the grasses. He did not lock the
doors of the cow byre or his herder's hut
but left the strings always unattached and
he counted the cows in by the noise of

their bells. He counted the cows by the noise of their bells and it was a little concerto for air and cow dialect sounding between his ears and its crescendos were aligned to the paces of walking and his breaths were accounted by the sun, his voice that fell against the hospices of rock. He stayed there and he made cheese, flicking milk with the whisk of the wood, watching it thicken and spiral like the lungs of water that live inside a hill. His legs were brown and wiry and he moved all the time like a drunk man who is always sober and he kept the stalls clean for the cows, manoeuvring shit into pits and drains. He trudged to Bernina, to Presena and Bernina and he walked all the high slopes in search of cows whose flanks were milk-brown. He called out to the bells, little bronzed udders, and they answered with ear-flicked words. Beyond the final houses, beyond the wild raspberries, beneath the pelt of the sky, beneath its thick furs, beneath the glistening skin, beneath the translucent void, close to the herbs of speech. Bread. Bread with aniseed and coffee. Bread hung on the high beams to dry. Dry bread and dipped coffee. Wine. Wine carried high in flasks. Cheese. Cheese of the mountain, as many kilos as he could. Herbs. Herbs flicked by cow-tails. And when the October snows came he brought the last cows down. And whenever he could during winter he went back up to Motta Varuna's snowline because snow is a moveable feast. That cowherd was me, grandfather. And before me it was Gaetano. And before Gaetano it was Emilio. And before Emilio it was you, grandfather. Slowly, slowly and then in fast rage the car goes off to Zurich or Milan. It is two hundred fifty kilometres to Zurich, to Milan. The car goes there fast, but is pulled apart by the journey. It is quiet now above Motta Varuna. It is time now for me to come down. For sure, it is time for me to come down.

Journey Across Breath

I can hear a man walking in front of
me down the slabbed road. That
should not surprise me. Nothing
should surprise me in this sharp
attenuated air. I know who it is : it is
you, nonno, going in your hobbled
boots on the uncambered roadway
down from Precasaglio to the town of
Ponte. You are just entering the
town's edge, going past the first stone
house. Soon you will go through the
gap where the road forms the ground
floor of the arched house. I know
without the shadow of a doubt that it
is you and you are twenty-two years
old and you have just decided
suddenly and in finality that you must
leave these mountains and go. Painful
that decision : but also without pain,
holding the complexity of a world in
one body and soul. But it never
flickered through you then, that I
would have to come and find you
almost ninety years later. I can hear
you, nonno, a handful of metres in
front of me. Your footfalls ring out
from the cold flags. I can almost reach
out and touch you, yet always you just
elude me. It is firm but dreamlike, this
vision of migration, this startled
geography, this life stuttered with

sudden clarity. Are only dreams the most real, dreams and death ? Why does such invisible loss seem the most palpable ? Or does death release what is real while our being alive is but a coursing of pretence and sleep ? Even these sharp and lovely moments of lucidity during daytime lives have to be likened to tiny deaths. Even though we love being alive and live our loves with passion. It is winter grandfather and you have just left the village of Precasaglio. You have just walked out of that bird-scooped cluster of houses hung above the raging river where young women wash clothes clean. Bird-scooped. You've walked the ridges and cart-ruts of the road. The snow-enclosed cemetery of the mountains. The church where your carved altar-rail still stands keeping separate the priest from his people. Past the flower-drained meadows and appendicitis fields. The road-fork at the church of Zoanno. The zag of the road going down to the workshop of the carpenter Ferrari. His turbid river at the corner still some distance out of Ponte. Along the narrow level in spate with the river you walk a hundred years before me and still I see you down the gradient as it plunges a little into the town (superb to look under the casual bridges and see the exploding waters). Under the floor of the road-arced house. Past the votive Virgin you painted when you were seventeen on the outer wall of Santini Giacomo's house. The oldest part of the town, changed little from how you knew it. That perhaps is why I am able to tear a gap through the veil of history and see you. That is why I can hear you now at this end of the final century and listen to the history of your migration at its beginning. That is why a little reality can flow back through me by the rip of its veil. I thought I would not be able to finish this fiction but now maybe I can. Or start it at least and let it ravel to reality. I can hear you there in front of me, the hob of your shoes spitting on austere flags. In front of me almost a century ago. What else should there be left to hear ? Is it as if sounds were still so air-struck and clear ? What has memory done ? Down one side of the valley everything freezes, down the other are villages, earth, bodies, stone, grass in sunlight. Sat in a cart and pulled by a horse I can hear you breathing. Your stuff of life. In no time you will reach Milan. Then time will spin backwards until you swivel through Paris and get to London. But, nonno, how can I talk to you when I never met you in my life ? How is this discourse possible and the only one that has sustained me through my tiny deaths ? Such moments of reality to lead to a sort of ecstasy. Such endings at the beginning that are always ...

* * *

There is a place above the last cluster of homes but before the final and sometimes inhabited *baita*, where the path crests a hill and flattens out a little and there is almost a small field of scorched tree stumps, where you know that something once happened, though quite what or when is not clear. There is an atmosphere of slight desolation, that is all, but it is enough to begin a story. It may have been where a number of friends, herders fetching sheep in the fourteenth century, were overtaken by a sudden and unexpected avalanche, sheep and dogs and herders scattered and four of the men killed outright, just smashed about. Or it may have been where the village priest, on his way down from the high *baite* having delivered unction to a dying parishioner three centuries later, was waylaid in the dusk going on dark by some bandit who thought him someone else and

who spent his own next twenty years
trying to resist the overwhelming
sense of guilt until he drowned himself
in icy waters unable to throw off at
last the black mood of despair. Or it
may have been that a middle-aged
mother one winter's afternoon
swooned by worry at the sudden
illness of her latest child carried the
babe wrapped in blankets down
toward the village but slipped on the
black ice of the path and cracked her
lowest vertebra, the two of them held
there in the gloom and savage frost of
the night, she dead in the morning
huddled over him and he moaning
slightly under her dead weight. Just so
we walk paths, like the lone traveller
in Dürer's winter scene getting past
the frozen pond and equally frozen
meadows while freezing birds drop
out of the sky and in a far distance the
white mountains glimpsed bring
unaccountable tears to our eyes, that
though we stop to watch even so we
inevitably carry on. Or it could have
been that partisans coming down off
the white zones of the war were
ambushed here by traitors of the
occupying force and killed not far
from their homes, or alternatively that
partisans ambushed their fellow
citizens of the different persuasion,
and that murders were done quickly

harshly and brutally leaving a savage
mess for dear ones to find, though the
partisanning must have been from
centuries gone since acts from but one
lifetime ago would have carried their
own clear story to our ears and eyes.
Or there as in the painting by
Brueghel we must have seen ravens in
the cold and grey air as travellers
passed by toward what burst stories
or shattered zones we could hardly
dare to imagine. What is it about time
that stops or in that place where the
slope evens out, flattening time totally,
and a patch of scorched stumps
indicate trees, trees that might almost
have been human. There in precisely
that place five thousand years back,
perhaps five thousand exactly for
all I know, a shaman left behind his
slaughtered son, wiped a reject of
blood on his face and his tongue and
walked the few hours up to the
hanging glacier by whose edge he
invoked geologies we can hardly
conjure and ate some parts of the
mushroom de magica right before
immersing his body in the fissure's
crevice, flaming with ice, from where
he was carried down all these years to
be deposited unambiguously and
clinically at our moraine's edge
flanked by trees that would be cut
down and burnt. Whichever or all of

these might have happened on this grass, there is an atmosphere here where the trees thin out to charred stumps, an aura that is strange to define ...

* * *

What happened to us in those years ? What happened in the interims that we have got to where we are now ? What happened after we'd established the family tree in the house of Annibale ? What happened to his son and his daughters who were well doing in school back then ? What happened to his nephews who drove lorries across Europe and his nieces who waited in their kitchens and domains ? How did it occur among the youth of those years that so many took to their veins dirty needles, that so many shared the communal fix from the goodness of their hearts, from the darkness of their bloods, from their urge to share and not to disdain each other. What happened to Annibale's son that his photograph got into the wall-niche of the snow cemetery before Annibale himself could get there. What white powders gave them succour in those bloated winters. Each

snowless day Annibale walks up past
Sankt Apollonia of the butters and
cheese to his baita where once Luigi
drove me in his four-wheel through ice
flows and frozen speckled pastures in
an astonishing scatter of driven skills.
There is a photograph of me on the
snow-path, grey-hair cropped,
walking shorts, a glass in my hand, a
smile on my face, a delight to have
held history in my hands, to have held
history back a short while and looked
four-square into its poor face. Every
written word is lost to time, it comes a
second, a minute, a century after
speech or act or the science of speech
acts or the violence of friendship or
the silence of snow. The last time I was
in Annibale's house in Precasaglio, we
had just come out of a little local
harvest gala in Gadda's church and
walked the thirty or so metres to
Annibale's blue door. There he
opened it and we went through into
his living room and in a while back to
the kitchen, the place where real
conversations happen, and we were
joined by many and no-one, and
stories blossomed from the beams and
dialect flowed and red wine and
salami and breads. This was another
gala, unrepeatable language in the
backroom of an old house, beyond the
power of speech, beyond the confines

of politics. This is what can only be
interrupted by time or assassination
or white powder or the poverty of
capitalism in the heart. All of us
gathered in the small room, no-one on
ceremony, no-one caring about
pretence or appearance, all as we were
with song and talk. But what
happened in those years, that span
between the appearance of the family
tree in Annibale's front room and the
gala of shared speech in the back one ?
What in the boredom of village
winters, in the archive of repudiated
histories, in the hands that throttle
time, what in the parasitic visitations
of the rich and infamous or the
parabolas of war, what in all this
drove the children to white powders
and a sweet share-out of contaminated
needles ? What drove them to deal
and fix in the brown sugars of glad
time ? The last I saw of Annibale he
was walking fixedly in the summer
sun, past the meadows beyond
Precasaglio where old women in blue
work-shifts and shawls still raked hay
into tiny wains in the first years of the
twenty-first century : Annibale on his
way again to the *baite* and the
storehouse of memory, lament maybe
in his mind but more than that the
sanguine knowledge of our lives and
celebration of the galas of language

and commune. My grandfather had walked there a century before arm in arm with his contemporary the Pezzo priest, and no doubt the same had flowered through their minds and hearts, for what changes in the micas of blood, or the flakes of sperm or of kissing eggs, or the white powders of contaminated time ?

* * *

In August 1920 when my grandfather returned to Precasaglio for the first time from London after the war and for the first time all told in seven years, there were two letters at his brother's house addressed to Longhi Bortolo from the then little-known Carlo Emilio Gadda. The first was postmarked Krasji and dated October 1917, the other from Milan in August of 1919. They had not been answered and it fell to Sebastiano to send a reply. Thus began the correspondence between Gadda and my grandfather that only ceased with my grandfather's sudden death from a brain haemorrhage five years later. What happened to those letters I'm not sure, beyond the fact that I found some odd lines, phrases, paragraphs

and jottings in an envelope of diary
entries and fragments that seem to be
in my grandfather's hand. They do
not at first sight say a great deal,
crammed in as they are with
stocklists, milk quotas, accounts and
other figures and brief lists of unusual
English words that my grandfather
was probably trying to familiarise
himself with. Neither, as far as I can
tell, is there any record in the Gadda
archives of this correspondence –
which is a little surprising given the
range of scholarship and recent
Gadda studies that have proliferated
everywhere and the fact that a good
deal of his correspondence (for
instance that with Bonaventura
Tecchi and with Eva Maria Sinistri)
has already been published.
Perhaps the letters from my
grandfather did not seem to matter
sufficiently to be kept : yet I don't
think that is the case. Rather I might
guess that there was something in the
letters, and in the copies of his own
that Gadda usually kept, that led
someone, maybe even Gadda himself,
to throw out or destroy the whole
bundle of the correspondence. At any
rate what cannot be doubted is that
during the week 18–25 November
1915, when Carlo Emilio Gadda was
stationed in the village of Precasaglio

during his time in the Alta Valcamonica, as his published diaries attest, he passed by on foot and subsequently met with the young man called Longhi Bortolo and struck up some sort of an acquaintance with him and that he remembered this meeting at a later date. Indeed he wrote at least these two letters, or they may perhaps have been postcards, with his characteristic drawings on them, to my grandfather's cousin Bortolo in Precasaglio, unaware that Bortolo had died in January 1919 when, having survived the whole war and fought in the campaigns of the white war in the mountains above Temù, his appendix had burst and no doctor had been able to make it through the severe blizzards and high snow meadows to his home in what was a month of severe winter storm. My mother remembers Bortolo – a lovely young man she said – twenty two or twenty three in 1918 when she, a twelve year old, came up through Edolo to Ponte di Legno in the first weeks after the end of the Austro-Italian war & entered the bomb-pocked town.

* * *

Nonno, didn't you love trees as much
as I love trees ? I'm sure you must
have done. You must have walked up
beyond Canè or up Gran Viso and
gone through thinning trees until the
last few remain stormed in late spring
by white horses. Look, this is a matter
of meditation, of meditation where
time stands still and whole worlds can
be sucked in or out of white and black
holes ! This is what history is, not the
batter of commerce, not the mass
murder of innocents by imbeciles, not
the constraint of hope by injunction.
Trees turn into people and people into
trees, as surely as a sleeping man in
his troubles becomes a cockroach.
Haven't you seen high spruce bent
slightly in the wind in the final
meadows near the tree-line, how they
sway and soak into bone and skin,
how they moan and dance into blood
and heart, how the bole is like a tower
of blood and bone is meshed into the
memory of bark. Dear heart, we
destroy trees for our own peril.
Or can I describe for you a circle of
sycamores in St. James's Park : how
their great bowl of air swirls and
dances, how their always-smaller-
becoming arms and branches
capillary themselves in the fortunate
air. Here between the halls of a
parliament and a banal regal house

we can squeeze out a free space for
breath ! Or in the old oaks and
blackthorn of Hyde Park, or a single
lost tree beside the Thames. Or the
superb deciduous woodlands on the
borders of Easter Sutherland and
Easter Ross, or the spring festival in
Glen Lyon. I once stood up through
the roof of a car moving slowly
through stands of old larch in West
Lothian. I once was mesmerised
by a single white-thorn at a junction
of the Ochil Hills. I once was unable
to leave sight of a single stately holm
oak not far from Stroud until my
friends half-dragged me silent away.
And I'm talking now just of the trees
of one island ! Think of the trees in the
Alps. Or those trees by the railway in
Satyajit Ray, in Tagore, or the flayed
riverrine memory of Ritwik Ghatak &
others in places I've never been able
to go. One time, Nonno, I lived three
years on an island without trees ! And
it was so, so beautiful ! An island and
a moorland and a bandaged sun !
Always a bandaged sun ! And a
moorland made from decayed trees, a
shepherd's cloak of peat laid down on
scoured ancient rock, across the scar-
line of mountains, on schists cooled
from the heat of magmas at great
depths, on little protuberances amid
the rocking seas. Our history, a seat

beneath a bandaged sun : from galaxy
to gaeltacht, from binary codes to
baita, veins and capillaries mapped in
the skies, models of life in the code of a
leaf, the colours of butterflies' wings
more complex than even our eyes.
That is why, Nonno. That is why it all
matters : your being born in the
mountains and then your leaving the
mountains and your life in a new city,
with all the global tinynesses in
between. If I write these things in both
joy and despair, it may be because
I've not eaten enough these past days,
months and years, please forgive me.

* * *

Hey, nonno. There must be a
predisposition among us lunatics not
to appear human. But we are. I can
assure you. Do you remember the man
on a summer's night on one of the
edges of Milano Stazione Centrale
who defecated ... And then turned to
the few onlookers, the passers-by and
said "look, this is me, this is what's
come out of me, this is what I have
given and what I have rejected, you
shits". Do you remember him ? Or the
lines of soldiers stamping in poverty
and cold on the streets of Tirano and

Sondrio who I saw years later in photographs on the walls of the café at Tirano Station having just arrived daytime from Zurigo ? Were they the lunatics, or was it the ministers and operators of the governments who best fit that word ? Shall we enmangle language to satisfy a failed dream ? Do you know how a tree appears to a lunatic on a summer's day on the altipiano ? No, I'll tell you, it is as a body swaying in the wind, bent slightly according to the pressure exerted by the earth's stress, a body transforming between a tree and a person, both the one and neither at the same time. But the lunatics, you know, know the abject stupidity of ever drawing boundaries & I'd rather go with the lunatics on that as with most things. My friend Manto has a superb story, probably you've not heard of it, you being born so European, about the exchange of lunatics between the partitioned governments of India & Pakistan in the late 1940s. Toba Tek Singh from between lines of barbed wire saying : "I am here, but where is my country ?" Seven pages of pure quotidian magic. I once saw a writ from some minister of ordnance & justice in your country banning all use of mountain language and the study or acclaim thereof. And once I tried to subvert a border guard with a flower, but of course it didn't work. The long journey of exchange I was taken on involved a bivouac of white words on a narrow road to the far north : lunatic and guard in easy connivance, a sphagnum of breath-laughter, until the final valley of snow streams and wild horses. Bird-flight is music and the journey made across breath is seen to be from one prison-house to another. Bird-flight is music, language is freedom, breath is laughter. And the perception of the lunatics that wherever they are taken is always a prison-house is a statement of the most exacted truth. Nonno, do you remember the sound your clogs made on the winter slabs before the war began ? But I say to you, what is the greater insanity : the appearance and behaviour of those we name insane, or the fact that languages and freedoms are suppressed, enmeshed in noise, polluted by government, dulled and denied ? What is the song of an old woman compared to the bonuses of a city banker ? But I know which I'd rather hear. And then silence – that lovely sonata between music and the eye – silence is compromised, made to be taken only as the ultimate option in the face of unbearable angers and

betrayal ? So, nonno, I hear your
footfalls ahead of me rocking against
the scroll of brown time ...

* * *

If I were to try to describe Silvi's
house, I would find it almost
impossible, though in some ways it is
not unlike my own home in London.
But Silvi's is on the outskirts of the
mountain town, really outside it on the
main road that runs above the village
of Pontagna, the cluster of houses
where Silvi was born. It is a large
house, not only the basement for
storing cheese and salamis but two
storeys and a loft in addition to the
ground floor and all the rooms high-
ceilinged. Moreover each floor has
four rooms and to the side there is a
yard and stables and hutments and
enclosed chicken runs and covered
corners. Silvi's father had it built in
1919, a strange time after the war and
used it not only to house their family,
including at times uncles and aunts
and cousins, but also as the office and
stage post for the carts and horse-
trucks he ferried goods with between
the railhead at Edolo and the town of
Ponte. Probably the war had served

him quite well, with all the soldiering and trade that Gadda refers to in his Giornale di Guerra. There is a photograph from the workshop of Pino Veclani dating I imagine from the early 1920s, a sepia print of three shepherds leading a flock of sheep along the road away from Ponte. Silvi's house is in the near mid-distance, perhaps two hundred metres behind the sheep, standing on its own in the morning sunlight and its huge sloping outhouses in shadow and cool for storage. It is stood there in wide isolation starkly but warmly and in total contrast to its present setting since the whole road on both sides is now crammed with modern and expensive houses. Indeed Silvi's house that must now be sold is also today expensive and in a way that would have dumbfounded Silvi and her father since the whole impoverished upper valley has been transformed by the tourisms of skiing. But it is not this makes Silvi's house so extraordinary, but rather the fact that it is almost wholly unchanged inside from the mid-1950s and in some ways totally unchanged from when it was first built over eighty years ago. Because Silvi after the death of her mother in 1964 never threw a single thing out : what couldn't be given to the pigs or chickens or manured for the vegetable garden or stored in the cool of the basement or burnt in the fireplaces, what couldn't be disposed of naturally or given away was, in its entirety and its complex quotidian variety, simply left in her home. In this way many rooms retained their ancient beds only one of which Silvi slept in and that in a room piled high with clothes and old clothes and furniture. The yard retained its ancient farm and garden implements, its harnesses and halters, its cheese packs and butter churns, its sheep bells and bum-shaped tractor seats, its horse tackle and its horse, for Silvi lived on there with the animals. If an inventory were made – or the attempt at – of the contents of Silvi's house even now five years after her death and in its empty months before any final sale, if an inventory were to be made a whole domestic and social history of the past century would ravel and unwind and furl itself into the openness of our faulty senses. But the house now must be sold, because Silvi in her years of abandoning her home and her self, in her years of sadness and her years of work, in her years of giving & grieving & giving, forgot to give her home to her nearest dearest and thus the house – far from being upkept in its most pristine disorder of

abandoned disinterest – must be sold
for the purpose of legal equality and
with regard to long-left sisters in
Vienna and Graz.

* * *

Nonno, I am walking behind you. You
are walking down Frith Street. You
are holding by the hand a young girl,
perhaps six years old. She is your
elder daughter and she is my mother,
and you go into the café at No. 13. I
follow you in. I am the young man in a
woollen hat who looks across at you
from time to time and who you are
absently gazing over at. I remind you
of a Polish or Catalan anarchist,
but more likely I am an Iranian
revolutionary from the time of
Mussadegh. For how long will
anything last ? It seems I am much
older than my mother. It seems I see
her across the café air and she is a
brave little girl. I say to myself "there
is my mother and she is hardly past
six". Claustrophobic in the corner of
the table. From time to time you look
across at me and increasingly the
shadow of a worry passes across your
smile. Only some time later will it
occur to you how appalled you were

by my presence, fear at a politics you didn't really know, despite Malatesta. You are thinking how difficult it is to get good waiters these days, you are saying as much to Gaetano Crammeri who comes from the same village and almost the same house as your wife in Switzerland. "If you could find for me just two good waiters ...". Nonno, I am walking behind you and you are perturbed. Because the blue bag slung across my back might not contain its wet fish and ginger, its ciabatta and fresh pasta that I am carrying for my mother eighty years later. I will cook it, pasta and fish with some tarragon when I get to her house. From the wine shop on Old Compton Street. God knows what fruits of the market may grow in our hearts. But I am interested only in you and in the girl who is going to be my mother. And for now, while I am intently observing the art and craft of your posture and conversation, you are drinking coffee with a finger of grappa and trying to fathom the credentials of possible waiters with your friend Crammeri. Your daughter is bored by all your business and talk. Dreadfully bored and she cannot stand cafés and moreover she cannot understand your Italian, much less the dialects you are trading with Gaetano. She is trapped by you against the café's walls, between the table and bench back without even a window to look out from and you have forgotten her existence there. "Papa" she is trying to say but cannot. Curt and rapid sentences splinter about her and you have misheard her caged voice. I from across the tables can smell hay and cow's breath and meadow flowers and I know that something will break inside her soon. Something from that array will wet her a very little, unexpectedly, and she will whimper a few steps on the way home. Still young, from here will grow a great need to be alone, together with a yearning not to be when she is. Sewn tightly inside her and then petalling open. I am the anarchist from the year 1912. Nonno, you are going out again into Frith Street and I too will get up in a few minutes. You will buy pasta, some tagliatelle, wine, tarragon, tomatoes, mountain cheese. And a brown coat for my mother, just in time you remember Nina had told you to pick it up from Arturo's. And now she is sitting here in her eighty-sixth year with myself the anarchist at this other table. We are under a cherry tree in the mountain town, under the cherry tree planted in the front fork of the garden of Hotel Pineta, looking

out into brown time, talking a little to
the waitress who has brought us some
tea and whose English is broken but
not broken too far ...

* * *

I drove sheep down from the
mountains, Nonno. I drove sheep
down off the rock crests and off the
sharp slopes. I drove them without
dogs. In small numbers as they were,
five or six at a time. I was able to do
that. I had that ability. That
confidence. I was nineteen, twenty.
Ages you were when you were still
shepherding in the Alps. I would go
out and find a few strayed sheep and
gather them together and drive them
down to the fank or to the pens behind
the hut. It was on the islands. Out
beyond Skye. Out in the sea. The east
side of North Uist. Schists and gneisses
that were near on four thousand
million years there. Astonishing
remnants. Geologies that I felt in my
body. Black pseudotachylites that
flowed down off ridges. I've not been
back in twenty-five years. What does
that matter. People were driven from
those shores a century and a half ago.
Cleared. More. Years even before you

were born. Put away for sheep to St.
John's or Newfoundland or Tasmania.
Much the same as you though :
leaving the land and migrating.
Sometimes across a small island from
one side to the other. Sometimes
across a sea. Sometimes from the
stretto of high valleys to the depths of
huge cities. From the nomadic lie of an
intuition or the tensions of an
economy irrevocably breaking down. I
drove sheep down off the mountains,
nonno. Like you, though I did not
realise that until years later. I went
and found sheep that had stayed out
all winter behind the mountain or that
had ventured in summer to all the
points of the peninsula. One time I
went as far as Bàgh Mòrag and sensed
seven sheep on a far neck of land and
drove them back close to the shore
four hours until we were back at the
home pasture. Another time we went
out to the ram's island at the edge of
the sea & I jumped down beside the
ram from a rock & held his horns to
secure him at the same moment. A big
drift-boat that to cart plenty of sheep.
That was a far rim of Europe, nonno.
That was a sharp place to fall off the
edge of. I wish I'd kept a journal of
those days : I'd read it to you now in
your haven of exhaustion. I would
remember with a proper blessing all

the grace notes in your life. Otters
rose in sea pools to watch movement
on the shore. Owls flew near my face
on the moor crests at dusk. A sudden
cleft in the treeless island had a rowan
    bush and a floor of gull-sewn
bluebells. Bog cottons and myrtle that
transformed the meadows and moors.
    I stayed there three years, my
university. But it was harsh what was
done to the language. Harsh what the
mother tongue had been put through.
Harsh what winters of imperialism
did. Nonno, wasn't that a nomadic
century in a time of comfort. If I were
to walk from North Uist to the Alta
Valcamonica, from the eastern shore
of a western island to the last high
    village in a European snowstorm,
what languages would I not learn on
the way. And if I went via Drohobycz.
And if I went through Olomouc. And
    if I went by Yerevan. And if I went
    with Rumi of Tabriz. And if I went
    with my son. And if I carried my
daughter. And if I went without guns.
    And if I went via Nellore. And if I
went by Chennai. And if stayed places
along the way. What languages would
    I not learn with these journeyings.
What words would I not arrive with at
the place of negative theologies. And
    what calmnesses could I not share
    down the last days of our lives. We

drove sheep down off the mountains
and a century passed by in the blink
of one eye.

* * *

Nonno, I had a dream. Fire destroys
memory and memory is overwhelmed
by flames. I dreamt that fires were
raging across the whole of Europe.
They were preceded by months of
spring drought and at first there were
isolated forest and scrubland fires in
parched parts of Portugal and Italy
and southern France. But then they
spread and became more continuous,
both in time and space. By the middle
of August the whole continent seemed
one fiery inferno : or black scorched
on brown. Even the parched boglands
of Tipperary and Cashel treeless as
they were had scorched and burning
mosses and top-peat. Even the
northernmost treelines of Scandinavia
and the high Alps & Pyrenees were
reduced to stir-pots of ash & a dried
grey scum. Cities were not spared. I
thought as I dreamt this that there
must have been signs or precedents &
I recalled fires on Sardinia & Corsica,
fires on Majorca & in the wooded
hinterlands of Lisbon, trees struck

down by lightning in the high Alps or
remote Scottish Highlands, stark
tree stumps in the midst of mild
fields, larch electrocuted to charcoal
on the altipiani, trees becoming people
& people becoming trees at the
heart of our terrifying century. I
thought of the National Library in
Sarajevo bomb-burnt to rubble
& of the solitary cellist playing
chords on huge scar-lumps of stone
& I thought of all the times fires
had been lit across Europe in
desperate attempts to keep warm. I
thought of the dream some mind-
madman – maybe it had been Jung in
his beatific calm – had had in the
months before war, of a great flood of
yellow water rising up around the
Alps and engulfing even them. And I
thought of the waters of the Vltava,
Danube and Elbe-Labe – alter-egos to
fire, sisters in love and destruction –
rising through their cities of Praha
and Dresden and Budapest and
wreaking their havoc and damage.
Fire destroys memory, nonno, fire
destroys everything and of a sudden
nothing is left. Even the superb and
ancient forests of Lithuania, their
inland corals and seas were reduced to
a ravine of steaming stumps. Even the
oak and elm of Moravia, the spruce
and larch of Sweden. Olive trees in

Sicilia and Campania, dry enough in their summer seasons, were blackened scars on a violet sky. The beautiful trees of Swaledale and Norfolk gone to blurry wind-scarred remnants. Even the *baite* in the mountains, nonno, even their trees and their dwarf-birch above the tree-lines. Mushrooms, wild strawberries, snakes, many many birds, all that had accumulated in thousands on thousands of years of balance and chance. Nothing was left, nothing and no-one. In the face of such terror language loses all relevance and ceases to matter and who is there left to speak or to speak with ? And yet what else can we hang on to ? Or are we such small print and prick on life that earth will hardly notice our going, and maybe celebrate as much as lament. Nonno, I crave to have another dream ...

VI.

How To Describe A Tree At Night

Arghezi Variations

Tinca (After Tudor Arghezi)

Her hip-basket of
sunlight propped on her thigh,
her pannier of sheaves with yellow
eyes & lashes, her milky
flowers, and night carnations,
her breasts & their black berries
tricked men's angel pride, her cries
"who'll buy flowers off the bride?"

Tell us, Tinca, tell
silky slippers, earrings, beaded ease,
Nastase didn't give you all these,
and every ring on every finger
did Nastase put all of them there?

So who did you let knead your ebony flesh
drinking back your fake, derisive sighs?
Who did you lie down with, threshing
the royal form of your formless thighs?

Who loosed your hair, stinking of smoke,
and pulled away your stockings & your slip?
Who was it buried your crazy, crackling head
with buckled sinews & arms about what bed
then shivered quietness to your bone of bones?

You never would tell anyone
where you spent your nights, you sweet-
smelling girl selling May gentians.

And now Nastase's inside for life.
He did only penetrate you the once but he
went right through to the shaft of his knife.

Rada (After Tudor Arghezi)

With a flower in her teeth
Rada is a wreath
of hot-thorned roadside roses
dancing in the rain-soaked soil.
She crouches, jumps, hoops her hands
she fritters joining-ropes of gold
and turns them into bridle-bits of foam.
She stoops her stiff back low
then bends her hip to throw her leg right back
toward the sky-flown starling flock
that's trapped silver in its star rack.

While jumping she had let us see
her flower, her red-black peony.
It seems the box that holds her stone of blood
was opened & then fell shut again. I would
like to bring my mouth down there & suck ...

I would like to nail
her amber statue, as a blacksmith
does fillies lying on the ground
that too moaned when they were downed.

Aiee, mother, tell her not to dance
or make water lilies of her flesh
or willows seeded by horse & chance.
I am ill with scent too strong for me
I'm sick with song that makes me groan,
Mother, do not let her dance – or, no –
let her come & dance & lie & moan.

Corrupt Words (After Tudor Arghezi)

All my
words are crooked,
awry scrawls, got so dead
drunk they have to crawl,
far away when near at hand,
slumped, got up, sumped down again,
wanting to run with energy
but lolled around the floors,
crackle, kink, are erratic, shrill
too much laughter's made them ill.

They got corrupted on their own.
They ran through swamps on gala days
hoping to get to the holiday zone –
my mildew flowers & fairground sprays
the daubed signs of my blunt claws.

Don't touch my words any more.
Don't let your lips move easily
on hissing sound. Nothing's proved.
Soar. Or sour. Or seer. Or sore.
Don't bring them here for song or
pamper them with rhymed music.

Gobshite! They make me sick.

Epiphany Under A Tree

As I lay on my back
the circle of trees formed a membrane above me
and light poured through the membrane
like egg yolk breaking from its broken sac
but none of the yellow sun touched me,
simply it gave me light.

I saw you there – your body was singing
your body was a stem swaying where you were
even though I broke the stem you remained intact
even though the stem was broke it gave me light

The stem of the tree moved to its finite twigs
light burst all over the face of the earth & my face
the trunk remained strong but burst to its limits
the membrane was stretched – the sky's membrane –
and light came through
where the yellow sun touched me
it gave me light

Beneath the membrane of trees
where the stem was singing in the layers of sunlight
the earth broke clear of its moorings & of me
and I grasped the chemical invasion of the stems
of impoverished speech

How To Describe A Tree At Night

To stand under a circle of trees.
To stand beneath the infinite al-gebr of dreams.
To be spiked on the logic of failure & of loss.
Leaves brush my face as I pass on inwards.
Trees are like inverted lungs & I breathe in.
Traffic is like a procession of ants – but without
                              ants' purpose.
The shrieks of geese, the calligraphy of branches,
            white writing against the sky.
The slight falling in of dead leaves in spring.
I stand under a circle of trees & breathe with
            the lungs of the earth.
For how much longer will this last ?
Is this how I can best describe a tree at night ?
            As if I stand in front of
Foxgloves & they are taller than myself. Yes.
This is my body. Yes. The one that is dissolved
            in sap. Yes.
This is my heart growing from inscribed valves.
And I should watch the kaleidoscope of wind-
            migrated leaves.
And I should reckon on the silence of my mouth
            of rooted speech.

August Sun, Passo Di Gavia

August in the northern sun.
And snow curling down the pine spurs
sewing wet dust into the nerve of spruce.
The next day we drove high into Passo di
Gavia along ice wreiths and raw surfaces
to the baitone of the blue & white lakes.
Wearing old boots and my coat flung off
my white vest loosened to the stilled blue
I ran stomping my footprints in the snow
up to the blue glaze of the sun's dead eye
high into the silent place of light and air
until a sudden edge would plunge me off.
Then I turned & walked slowly back down
my footmarks to where the streams were
turning into water and standing trees. Up
on the other side was the Tre Signori and
its plumed cornice in a silence of hawks.
We had grappa and salami at the ice edge.
My mother played here sixty years before
& partisans were gunned down in the War.
Then we drove back the long way round
above the ravines where Giacomo used to
herd sheep as a child on the other side &
in a great loop we got back to the Pineta.
I went down 3,000 metres in a short hour
and it broke open my memory & passed
me through the ur-starts of dead language
an unriveted congestion of stretched time.
My mind fell into that glacier and it was
Only spat out these thousand years later.
Ah Dolor ! I have tried to assassinate my

own tongue & I have not managed it yet !
& the photographs you took there of me
with your father & Luigi & Ennio have
disappeared in the muds of brown time.

Via Glori

There, where the slabbed
and melting road slowly unfurls
its water channel to the city's edge,
and the radiant and quotidian city
stands a moment gasping in the haze
of the solitary sun, until the raw sun
becomes a small boy who stands up
on his bike to ride in slurred motion
through the crossroads and final bend
out past the maize fields – but the sun
is a basin of steaming polenta slapped
on the scrubbed table of a white city –
and this boy sees all this rushing by :
the maize fields and the wild cherry,
chicory on the knife-bone of red time,
tomato stems on the sun-slopped wall,
each growing fruit a tiny sun with an
urgent lack of diffidence in its blood,
there where the road finally threaded
through the encircling highway away
to a tree and house of wooden clogs &
sadness is the foreground sucked back
in the sickness of his glutted energies,
there in the spindly path of Via Glori
from the white densities of wall to the
mountain's unsordid name – as if all
of life will go on for us too – and the
high pass is tensed by sudden snows
and the sun's tiny oranges fall among
lime and clay and we are the earth's
objects for which no time is allotted,

and narrative in the summer city is
melted by the lovely logic of the sun,
there, where the boy is a clay tongue
in the city's great bell, in the days
before ever he cooled to bronze.

VII.

80s Poems

A Birth-Song

I was born from a birth-cone
from a cervix, from a womb
I came out with blood & with
stupor from a pulsing vagina

I came out when she had come
inside & out of her womb blood
and I thought the sun was alive
beating our earth with breath

I came out covered with blood
good it was – wasn't it good !
As with the generous, powerful
serene bloods of menstruation

I put praises on these words
pour praises over them I do
first blood and womb blood
and I see the sun's wet face

Dancing and screaming just as
she was dancing and screaming
good it was, wasn't it good –
come from the womb with blood

With black and with red blood
I came out like a dear animal
from a cervix, from a womb –
bright from a pulsing vagina.

Clarinets Of The Sun

Power Of The Powerless
Vaclav Havel

There is a buzzing in the silence, all
the clothes, all the poor rugs & pillows
caved about our heads could not muffle
this noise, the noise of the powerful,
    the noise of their power

And behind that sound is a silence,
through that silence another sound comes.
It is a relic hum, hum of the humiliated,
of you and me, trying to shake the dusts
    from off our caking eyes

It fulled the air about our static faces.
And as asbestos falls from factory walls,
it drifts – this buzzing – into everywhere
& yet our muffled hum is never dulled
    inside of slow enchanted time

And as a city is – in its liquid nights –
with tower blocks asleep in pastel gowns,
at dawn beaked blackbirds burst the light
and carless streets can smell of apricot
    and baked sweetcorn

And the strangest thing – as is birdsong –
is our remnant humming will sing through.
Power of the powerless – such time is come,
within its hum our struggle sings, this is
    the clarinet song of the sun.

In Memory Of Egishe Charents

My irreplaceable friends were being felled
Egishe Charents

How friends peel away, not
that they die, physically in any
of the measurable senses we know,
but how they peel away and die –
those of immense intelligence who
talk & can talk only of themselves,
those who can only love in couples
& yet can hate in their thousands :
we who can't conform to such life,
how we are killed off even before
we die, lost amid speech & reason.
I know it's not necessary to struggle
any longer on this earth for love –
A dark dolphin with red & yellow
fish swirling in its belly, this earth,
swung round in all its slow circles.
Fresco of the city painted by red
fingers, inside my veins. Head
crushed on a wall. Sheep's tripe
soup drunk early so as to ward off
drunkenness. Earth hung in mid-
air. My irreplaceable friends are
destroying themselves, and those
tired ones who from lack of love
bite off their own fingers. It's in
children's drawings & the words
of their play, their yarded games
& the clemencies of open hearts
that might be found the necessity
to struggle for love, or the only
loving that is left us on earth.

Eid Mubarak

As I cross the road
under the railway arch
this ice cold night of Eid

Four or five lads cry out
from their mobiles : 'Apples
& pears, give us a bite'

And it's true I was biting
a pear down to its string
against the stone of night

Later, later when I've
got to Hanbury Street
I'll remember the core

Of a voice ached in ice
that only when naked can
the cold seem to be warm

And the gondola slice moon
as it fell away off that face
so early in the morning.

Explanation

Mylonites &
mashed gneisses run through
Eubhal & Beinn na 'h-Airidh
& solid streams of black tachylite
slide to calve their fabrics
in the open sea

Threatened with
being knocked from its axes
the earth looks with familiar
compassion on these broken teeth
remnants of the first mountains –
and with dye blue from its gums –
o most new of all old-new voices –
tries to soften out & full
the oppressed science
that speech is.

Fitting Words

My hands I walked – across your back
every vertebra – was a letter typeset
the 'a's & 'm's – were for your sleep
as opposite shoulders are for heads ...

And then the whole chanced-on typeface
rose to float on the air and look down –
the honeys of sleep in our blade bones
for the calm whirr of a breathing stone

Ah little sister with your bit red string
what happened between us is lovely & gone
your bag is still in the ship of my room
red and black flag for an unheard return

What stirred in us was an exile of blood
a republic we formed – but a monarchy too
words of typeface with a swirl in a nerve
the transient power of your way through

The red black flag is an anarchist flag
your bag is still in the ship of my room
honeys of strain were spilled in our eyes
what rose to float above & look down ...

There above everything – a great rigour
the type-holding tray of our being alive
sent with each breath – energy & vigour.
A pity ! We parted ! Good that we tried !

Hawking Radiation

From constrained fields
all matter flew outways,
all matter solidified,
that beetle & its small dung,
blue iris, trilobite head,
every glowing, curling fern,
dust & its infinities,
glacial grit and glacier,
all the faces we wash ourselves as, you & I,
all affirmation & denial,
all yessing & no-giving,
loveliness of the colour
black, black hole outwith
time, outwith space,
gravity that is measured,
what shines & nothing but,
& this immense fiction of
wondering whether any of
us will ever be needed
       again.

Joan Eardley

This is her house. Across from it
the sea and its crests of beehives.
The sea she held stilled with paint
the paint she made solid with sea

And the bees – the beehives – so
she understands the earth's axes
that buzzing & sudden silence are
the speech of those who can't talk

The sea is buzzing in her sleep – or
no – bees are sleeping in her hands
blue hives gathered on far horizons
swim in white air close to her shore

This is her house. Touch it again.
Paint it on the axis of her silence.
Not many like her have courteous
intuition, giving freedom to space.

Behind her home are stooks of corn
with blood nipples on blue stalks.
They are bairns from tall tenements
their eyes look right out into hers.

The air's a fishing-net left out to dry.
Sea-birds sew taut the skin of the sea.
Hem & grace of it. This that she did.
I'd want to make painted words fly.

A Kind Of Europe

Grasses spring up in my firstborn land :
in the mountains to the south sunlight
overwhelmed the snows & I waded through
until the crest fell off its sudden edge.

The occluded valley of the sleep herders
with trenches from the last but one war.
Mountain towns, their walls bomb-pocked
in the white slaughter of winter ascents.

There were small headstones by the road
where partisans had come down at dawn.
Words carved in schist beside rye fields
and read in memory of shattered homes.

We do not speak the words that are ours :
knives put through the throat to sustain.
Laugh at the baroque clemency of it all.
A half-century gone by without breath.

Workers returning from sulphur mines
walk to their towns of red-tiled rooves ...
A blackbird gasps its song from a branch.
Grasses sprout through the city roads ...

Far, far to the south a red lateen barge
sets sail for the island of salt & the mine
owner's niece slid down silk-white dunes
to enter the world of the bursting sun.

Marina's Nail

Marina's nail is on the back of the door
The train of Attila approaches the lake
Sergei's blood – he's been using it as ink
It's my abrupted voice trying to speak

The sun has sunk down the tobacco sky
The spine of our years is ripped away
The horses of speech are subtle & slow
It's my abrupted voice trying to say

European scorn has flowed out & stopped
The intellect's in control of the fertile mind
Let the flooded waters be dried in the sun
The blood, the heart & what can astound

On the crest of the road there was a shop
With yoghurts & cheese & aniseed loaves
On painted walls & in fields in the ruts
Translucent calm animals leapt in snows

The nail of Marina is there on the door
& Attila's train is approaching the shore
It's the blood of my voice trying to speak –
A translucent red animal crying out for
more ...

Poem For The Children Of Millbank School

Listen :

I am quite simply the poem where children without barriers
        draw & write, write & draw
    as if to write & to draw were the same thing –
        which, of course, they are

Look here is the face of Noorjehan, she's playing word games with me
she's making me repeat words & then giving me sudden properties :

        Jelly. Say 'jelly' Steve. Now you're
        Wobbly !

        Properties, mind. Not property.

I am quite simply the poem where I am no-one's property.

    Listen (but do not listen)
    to me : why should you listen to me when it is
        I should be listening to you !

Anyway, it could have happened that I was away in the mountains.

That I was away in the mountains walking up to Rifugio Bozzi.

Or that I was walking back down from Precasaglio to Ponte & hearing
the footfalls of my grandfather though it is the best part of a century
        since his feet walked out of that village for ever.

But I am not there. I'm sitting in the library at Millbank Primary Junior
School & across the table from me
Noorjehan is laughing at the trick she's played
('Steve, Steve ... now you're wobbly !')
and Julian is drawing his writing in slow cadence.

Soon we will get up to climb on the shelves & watch
the rest of the class through the windows playing
football in the playground before it can snow ...

We're getting ready to leave ourselves behind, to leave our lives

We're getting ready ...

My Mind Is A Wilderness ...

My mind is a wilderness
peopled in its time by raw flesh.
It has no computible apparitions.
My mind sings. Song has no end.
This must be that nightmare
someone will unleash me from.
My daughter died. My wife &
Son are gone. Jean is dead.
My father dead. My mother took
with grief & bewilderment.
Every logic hides the compassion
I'm far too unconfident to find.
No job. Cannot savour poetry.
Poetry cannot succour people.
Political hurt has hurt too far.
Sunlight. The building collapses.
Choice has leapt from my mind.
What without uncontrolledness
can a constricted mind achieve,
without control what can be held
fertile in the mind's cowed
                    space ?

Poem For Nichita Stanescu

You in the aftermath of rains
(in our Europe which is a mud bath)
in an autistic pullover & pair of jeans
are led across a real village wet street
by a peasant cloaked in red-blue pockets
from the carved circle of a wall as far as
the endless tower that is both love & death.
So, I see you calm in that plague column
drinking juices of language as you must,
and the juices of speech utter your words
as you burst now upon the void : only in
such a savage snowstorm could freedom
– that gentle barbarian – echo through
all our times like a dear erotic dialect,
skinned clean to the bone by kisses &
pulled back from the edge of oblivion.

The Face Of Nima Yushij Leans

The face of Nima Yushij leans across Iran
and not many people see him, only the dead
with their blood and their lucidity see him,
leaning right the way over the spine of Iran

And across Europe Nima Yushij leans his eye
and over America – for he's tall this Nima –
but almost no-one sees him there, some poets
or Ahmad Shamlu where in heaven he'd be

For he jutted out from the earth and was bony
and after his death he continued to grow tall,
a few hairs glimmered just above his forehead
curling in sympathy with the rim of the world

The huge bald rock of his head shone out, or
no – it was a risen crust of oven-baked bread.
Just so the doughs of the mountains are alive –
what raced in his veins were horses of blood.

When he died a furnace shut down in his skull
and in the city a crowd stopped & then roared.
The face of Nima Yushij leans out across Iran –
then turf it to a hot oven, o my village mother.

The mountains of Iran have roots in the air,
it is in their buckled depths they are human.
Once or twice he thought of this task of living
& shah & mullah were drenched in green air.

Walking Hand In Hand With Nunu Miah

If a child
has crumpled his body beneath
low chairs in the class & manages to lift
his head & then gets himself up on his legs,
sun-dazed as a licky colt that's just been born,
then you hug him to you & give him your hand
& walk in the summer densities of his playground
into the whirling spools of skip-song & sun-gonged
kids, their lives & ours a dance & a circling song,
and the red ball that's heaved high on the waste.
A cat is there when we go to retrieve that sun,
still as the struck bird it's baiting on the waste.
A summer season's passed in liquid intensities &
I'm still walking hand in hand with Nunu Miah
because much of his life is in its frozen quarter
& he's still steepling on the tight edge of speech.
The great coil of written words that could describe
the distraught erratic candour inside his mouth,
his small benumbed calm & downcast loveliness,
that coil's about to unwind if only there's time,
if only there is time it surely is about to unwind,
or if time could be a sun-gonged cat waiting
for the fever shift of vision just to pounce.

Self Preservation

Or not even that.

In a way like the donor in old paintings,

A lost figure in the corner of the canvas.

Or merely a name. Or a number. Or

                  nothing.

Sparrow dived by a kestrel at the open door

              of a blackhouse.

In the sunshine of this world.

A woman's hair like a paintbrush in its clasp.

The trails left by migrating insects.

An escutcheon of feathers trodden on by a

                 horse.

Or not even that.

One day I will emerge into the great sunlight

              of this earth.

Shopping For Honeys

Where the tower block is – was a church
on the site of Sainsbury's – a synagogue.
Cars left underground are under a school
three sisters went to seventy years ago ...

Meat or fish. Or bone or rice or juice.
Juice is good – in our bodies or in flasks.
Made from honey-apples or compassion-grin
as if we shop for love while wearing masks.

There is a ghost walks down Watney Street
Somehow the ghost keeps most of us alive.
Just so a bee from the river's city wharf
flies across water to its one known hive.

All of us make honeys – inside ourselves.
Some make love with honeys in their blood.
Others tilt compassion out their body's flask
& look amazed seeing swimmers in the flood.

The tall, the slim, the hurt, the poor, the fat,
the thin, the harmed, the happy & the dull :
who knows what any other body needs to have
walking round the market's cordoned hall.

In place of twisted roads – a market-place.
Flats like Buddha caves on a mountainside.
And all of us drink honeys, juice or beers
to float the die of living right out wide ...

Then Cook & Eat & Stand & Look

The shadows thrown across the grass
by sunlight running on pastured snow
each house picked out on the city's mask
& each one of us with nowhere to go

The white snows of daylight that woke us
in the mornings that woke us & woke us
go to the window breath on the glass pane
ice-flowers crystals candles to greet us

You would think that on a day like this
you could run on the roofs of the houses
you'd think that on a day such as this is
your veins had the blood of white horses

When I have opened my flesh to the sea
and have let the sea in to interpret me
then when all the interpretation's done
my flesh is glazed by the whitened sun

Our flesh is glazed – the sun can sing
we know the sun by the ache it can bring
suddenly the air drifts thick with snow
light comes back – light's quick to go

Walk to your home down the city's night
nerves in your belly – are a building site
then peel away down the hill of yourself
spit down the snow slope – your wealth

Your mimicry, that dark-shining lake
and all the city you've just had to take.
Then cook & eat & stand & look &
work & shit & dream & talk ...

Translucent Horses

Each poem is
a translucent horse, its
belly of blood lit up in
the white city of
      the sun

Each poem is
pulped fruit fermenting
in the guts of red horses
drunkenly trampling
      fruit trees

Each poem's a
meeting-place of people
where words leap over
rutted democracies
      of blood

Each poem is
as nothing compared to
the integral disorder of
all of us in the poem's
      bright hall

Each poem is
a blood orange, a lucky
organisation of words spilt
against the censure
       of people

Each poem is
the gap between indifference
& eternity : a translucent
horse leaping across
       into light

Winter Afternoon

(In Homage To Marguerite Duras)

When a god comes too close
the cormorant flies straight at the sun
the yellow bloodied egg of the winter sun
that injects its light into cages of dark
& stuns the land with its golden splash
& stains of bloody yellowish mauves.
Invertebrate that pillar of dark bone
that is my back when I feel it bite.
It's not enough simply to write words,
so supervising the activities of madness,
the sombre exultation of lives within,
barren regimes of love & cages of air,
dispassionate aviary where meanings are,
little fascisms of honey, exampled anger.
None of that is enough. Nor this rage.
The cormorant flies straight at the sun
& burning is not burnt but comes black
& uncharred to the ether side of light,
pushing its beak toward the pulverised
      winter islands where we are.

Whitechapel Muezzin

Summer Friday, one o'clock
the taped muezzin cracks the air.
Out across the hot dirt of traffic
Muslim men are walking to prayer.

Workers have gold-leaf-painted
the Jamme Masjid's great apple dome.
In the haze of our blue glowing city
Nazrul Islam is asleep in his room.

Big-jawed frozen fish are swimming
in the blue transparent air. Grandson
and grandfather eat off the one plate.
A hot knife burns the mother's tongue.

Where you can have tea & ghulabjham.
Where beigel sellers once sat to sell.
Abutting the Tower House doss home.
Where the great human traffic swells.

Mother tongue talks to mother tongue
and everything has its pattern. The sky's
a prayer-mat where the weaving shifts.
The child eats biryani, wants rasmallai.

Shaffique Uddin gets up in Settles Street
all of his village is clear in his dream.
The air round about the apple-gold dome
resounds to the call of the taped muezzin.

Little Poem On The Life Of Xiao Hong

Well, you fled to a north-eastern city –
The beautiful impoverished Manchurian
        town of Harbin –

What's important is what is elsewhere – you
Were not a camera to puncture your horizon –

You knew little peace in your life – the death of
Your grandfather & then the death of Lu Xun –

Tales of Hulan River, Field of Life & Death :
Most of your fictions were autobiographical &
You, the narrator, of secondary importance.
Like a description of weather in a place where
The thermometer plummets into solid ice – but
You in your fiction were a poet of destruction.
Your death at age thirty was not so unusual –
But I will miss what you did not write : & I'm
Wondering what history might have been if it
        hadn't been just as it was.

And I look at my contemporaries, the lists of
Best young poets, the 'new generation', those
    who seek plaudits to be given unasked :
You would be a little more than eighty now –
The age your grandfather was when he died –
After that you hunted yourself down without
Luck in your desperate quest for love & for
        human warmth.

William Heinesen On His Ninetieth

You looked like Ezra Pound,
but you aren't : striped shirt of a
seaman or shirt striped by semen –
as if all you had given through your
life were woven as solid white lines –
and the holy wanderer's stripey cap.
Your wife is beside you and you hold
her close, you with your shoes, you
with your stick, your cap, and your
brother dead since nineteen twenty.
I look at your eyes & see slits of red
gneiss where lucid shadows dance,
I look at your words and like Arctic
elegies they coil in my boned trance,
Like paper-thin rose terns they float
on storm crests, refuse solid ground.
The tower at the end of the world is
the deepest axis of all your calm and
spins where everything's gone silent.
Go there. Come back. It's too cold.
But you are gone & will not return.
Coil of bracken in curl of sea sand.
Now your wife is on her own. I see
her sitting over near the sea. It will
be her turn soon, but it seems to her
a fine ship has finally broken anchor
and passed quietly out in the night.

VIII.

Strands, Clusters ...

Twenty-Five Breath-Takes Walking Down The Swale

* 1

in each field
a suitable barn :

a beautiful light
is shed by work

* 2

(swale flow)

a bronze ribbon
on the field of snow

* 3

you cannot see the swell of the swale
unless you stand at the bridge's wall

* 4

you cannot see the river in spate
until you stand on the bridge and wait

*5

how many buttercups
in the swale meadows ?

how many mountain
orchids on the moor ?

*6

a hundred thousand
in a single field

constellated : a yellow
milky way

*7

broken walls
broken houses
broken clouds
warm sun

strong heart ...

*8

stone walls writing poetry
across the sides of the hills

* 9

hawthorn in
the middle of a hill field :
snow in early summer

* 10

the alders walking with the river
the river walking with the fells
the treading gone with that spate

* 11

you can't smell pale hawthorn
from the shut window of a car

you can't pick wild garlic
at forty miles an hour

* 12

language is
a slabbed path running
through flower meadows

* 13

what is the point of
language if you cannot say
things like this ?

* 14

walking the corpse path
streamers furling colours
far behind me

* 15

between the trod
and the force : pit-ponies
judder slacks of lead

* 16

fleecing
the storehouse of
language

fleecing
the store ...

* 17

bird-sing, lark-
song, shrike-
shriek

thief !

* 18

to leave the path
is the best path to
follow : leave it

* 19

clover growing
through buttercup
buttercup through
meadow grass

* 20

in evening dew
an adagio of flowers
loosens its scents

* 21

the sanity of
the mad is what keeps
me (from) going ...

* 22

(lark-song)

what is the
point of borders
when music listens
like this

* 23

(swift-flight)

million-yeared
aero-dynamic :

bird-brained
brain of a bird

* 24

(last one again)

swifts and
swallows leaping
constant tight-ropes :

it is the cliff
falls off its own
edge

* 25

no-one I
know is mad :

a beautiful light
is born of work

* (last one)

no-one I
know is mad

praise be your
name, no-one

Strands, Clusters ...

grew up in a village in Sylhet

that she knows and loves village life

"appa, how do you know that"

two strands

held together by language and commitment

through the language link

a whole life history in 15 minutes

talking with her this comes across as a lovely strength

itself is a lucid image of continued narrative

a strand of light

though these are my words

a part of the tapestry she carries within her

*

within three months of arriving

as the only child in the family with english

she began working with older women

again the day to day association between language and living

and she in her memory

returns to the language source

that her work is both vital and rewarding, its status both

recognised and not

this she knows

*

the language beyond the language

that in her language poetry is still important

that poetry is the form of first and deepest cultural expression

for love, sadness, illness, war

now anomalous in english :

that such a rich language should position poetry in this

abnormal, marginal place

*

his family was living in

the industrial town of

Chhatak in

north eastern Sylhet

a cement factory   using local limestone

and water from the Surma

as it comes down from the hills

of Assam

he

loves Nazrul and respects

and responds to Tagore

in a calmer way

*

& she smiled widely & said yes

      *

in the city of Jamshedpur

we talked quietly for an hour in the small downstairs room

she had grown up among many languages

calmly : feeling the sense of achievement

      *

trained as an actress

and then worked in the state theatre for 15 years

we talked a lot about Melih Cevdet

his long poem 'The Death Of A Vessel'

I remembered his superb lines where a boat is leaving

      the shore :

'the land was near at first, very near,

I could have touched it if I'd reached out my hand

the night that rose and fell was my starless ship

....

what rose and fell before me like the sea

was a god's artery.'

she trained as a linguist

she trained as a counsellor : never, never are you just

a translating machine

*

she loved going to the village as a child : freedom

"what is point of grammar if you can't speak the language"

she came to Tower Hamlets when she was thirteen

during night shifts she was often called on to translate

she feels proud of her achievements

giving emotional support as part of her job

from one to three : and more

not simply a matter of linguistic understanding but also

of confidence, eye-contact, social awareness, thus :

"listen & translate, listen & translate, listen & translate"

(but of course it is more than this)

*

and finally we talked about song

she likes *sangeet* very much

nazrul & rabindra *geet* : the lost day songs

she sings to her daughter

*

the mother was wearing a deep purple sari

the daughter had a history of stomach pains

*

had been in the children's hospital most of the time

since she was a week old

both parents were balanced and grateful and strong

facilitated by her professionalism and openness

both because of the ease of language communication

and because she had known them a long time

most of all their daughter's life

in a quiet and most impressive way

*

the mother lying next to her baby and later the way

she held her in her lap cross-legged

translating for a young woman doctor speaking

calmly and directly

she was living on the ward with her child

reassurance : the importance of that

the mother with the wee one in her lap

the understanding of the mother, the waiting, the arms,

the patience, the exhaustion

and this shared fact of language

*

that the work she does clearly matters

that her work enables her to put the patients first

and that is what she wants

that she is a language worker

I asked her who her favourite poet was and she

said : Rumi

she remembered something from deep in her

childhood

how her mother went every year to the city of

Konya

and returned home as it seemed to her daughter

from a place where language was

glowing with light

*

she has almost always worked with nurses

often the only non-nurse among nurses

a calm and lovely feel to her work

built up from solid commitment and story

somewhere in the gap between sociology and song

*

I come into work

I put on my work clothes

the patients depend on me

and what would they do

if I were not here

*

poor housing and

that winter of long-lying snow

sewn together with learning a new language :

although she had arrived with no English

within a year she was being asked to translate

and interpret for her family and in school

her face carries the light of

narrative and memory

＊

crucial

ongoing deep friendships

narrative strand :

having to say quickly   in loco parentis

that she was the elder sister not the mother

the yeast of giving I'd want to say

partly friends saying "you must make use of your

languages"

*

a young child in a village in the Panjab

calling her 'amaji'

etched into the language she grew up speaking

they lived close by the river Jhellum

her grandfather had crops (melons, groundnuts) on

the other side of the river

fields of sesame, trapping birds, being out on

the flat-roofed houses

where the sense of language and balance was

created

Discourse With The Physicists

It was not always like that. It always was.
Once we had strength & delicacy of lace &
where a straight line was, a cluster of curves,
a spiral of trajectories : the best way to reach
the point right in front being to set off backwards, a circle being a straight line. One time
there was a landscape of karst-off limestones
plunged to the sea and thus a string of islands
with the sun pouring its cogent goblets of raw
light over the earth and this was not paradise
but day's bright fact knotted in time and space.
Red arrows of corundum and blue tourmalines
and we have come from the first struck fission
from the simile of calm ether and its tolerance.
For this reason then we must touch warmth in
a body, with our fingers of tenderness unwrap
lines on the sleek under-skin. There were golds
there were reds and yellows, blues and greens
a sun poured its crimson wine from the goblet
of karst cliffs risen up from womb-wet waters :
a house was built, a house with its eight walls
they were carved with saint's faces, and with
the shapes of animals & birds & healing herbs
on its outward and on its inward vaulted roof
and with frescoes in the coolest inmost rooms.
Everything is in everything and everything is
plural : it is only in the aftermath that all pain
breaks loose, that villages are tossed off cliffs,
or severed heads are reaped as grape harvests,
that towns are moved across razored maps or

mountains rubbed from the face of the earth
or off our faces, for when is a face not human.
Red mountain of my village rising inside me.
Everything is plural and everything is in us.
Everything is a yes against the garnering no.
Or must we forget the physics of our own
disinterest, must we affect the dyslexia of
                our own physical storm ...

                          * * *

Shall I tell you about my mother. Or you tell
me about chaos. Word from the childhood of
Pirandello. Lateen-sailed barge full of young
girls that landed on an island south of Sicilia.
Daughters sliding down slopes of white sand
to celebrate the earliest years of that century.
Why ours though ? Why early ? Who said this ?
Boats sinking with their cargoes of refugees.
Humans laundered off Libyan coasts tossed
Wholesale onto sinking vessels left to drift.
Birdsong of the Somali boy collapsed by war.
Kaos in the breaking seas of the white sharks.
I shall show you a photograph of my mother
looking out at me from the year before zero.
And you will show me the turbulent flow of
fluids, time and the river, chaos and its knots,
matter with the delicacy and strength of lace
caught up in the hexagons of the then & now.
My mother's eyes filled with the sight of time,
century's white bow in her hair, starched yes,

and lineament of the loveliness of her mother.
Agosto veintetre giorno di nascita d'Costanz.
Nina awaiting the arrival of Celeste forever.
Tell me about the chaos of fluids, about those
boundaries beyond disorder, about your laws
that melt into silts on the other side of ether.
My grandfather sitting quite still and waiting
in the backroom of the Creamery for what on
earth will come. Haemorrhage that will wreck
him, clot of his brain that burnt holes through
the lives of his daughters, city stripped of life.
Thick curdling of variegated colours, churned
creams, time, and speech, and of all that ends.
Tell me about the fluidity of chaos, about how
it trawls against the muds of history and goes
    forever flowing through our veins ...

                    * * *

Sweet Europe. My dear Europa. My liar.
When a bird flew across the plains one day
midway in the term a terrified scream rose
pulling storms over the northern cities and
in its aftermath Europe clotted with silence.
Passage of a divined bird through blue and
golds of the Mediterranean and a shark sea
that is slowly losing the prime colour white.
This is a nocturne and this the morning star.
This constellation a map of the railways and
of autobahns and of jets in the trade stream.
Viruses of intensity in the last years of war.

This is the sunrise and this is the dark angel.
Betrothal and elegy for the charred beloved.
What inconsistencies make our love prosper.
What intricate stains in the heart of hearts ..
What mountains rising through our bloods ..
What collapsing at the fall of sandalled feet ..
Who of us has managed to risk everything ..
What else is there between our lives' clarity
and the friction of chance. In all our naïveté
love is like an atom : it can exist in incipient
space, it can erupt, it can glisten & then will
implode internally, or it can be plummeted
down the black hole we all know, O my
　　　　dear, O my sweet Europa ...

　　　　　　　　　* * *

We'll shake some words – or be shaken
by some – and place them whole for their
wide-eyed sisters and brothers. And blind
heated speech may say what we want it to.
Language was a hedgehog under the hut :
you had only to poke it with the end-stick
of summer and it'd come out into the light.
Language was a hedgehog under the hut :
a bright painted ball rolling in thick grass,
the eye of a child in the root of all daisies,
the curl of fern in the spiral of all wombs.
Language was magma deep in hot earth,
language was the horse blinded at birth.
If you find some Galileo seek out please

those pages where he speaks of the moon,
minutely describing it as a tangible thing
and with the words he uses his quotidian
mind is rarified to a gut of lucid levitation.
If you write a book about love and sorrow
call it 'The Little Geology Of My Era' or
'Seagone Bird' or whatever you may. Or
'A Little Primer For Burning Of Books'.
Even if books are what you love the most :
Especially if books are what you most love.
Be at home with the botanists because the
courage they had to study in the bleak time
on Lake Sevan when human heads bubbled
as if in terrible evocation of later volcanoes
made them value words as evocations of
a savaged freedom.

* * *

Only reach the end if you can rest in revolt.
Trust not those who tell you what to do, only
trust those who can no longer say what's true
or those who have abandoned all competition.
I'm come to this : a thin tube where particles
are being bombarded through light and time.
There is a hole in the wall it is no longer here.
There is a hole into what cannot possibly be.
There is a shimmering torn & flapping sheet
where our silenced world is being unfurled. It
is the silence between theology & our mutiny.
To reach here we have not gone by logical line.

To reach here we have set off backwards and
come in curved light until the circle arrives at
the place next in air to where we were. This is
the richest way to get here. This is how blood
for instance flows and we have gone sideways
through time and through all its possibilities.
We have followed a spiral trajectory to arrive
at a sea shore where spits of land are burning.
Cormorants fly straight into the sun and it is
our world unfurling in clouds of archetype or
compressed geologies. This is how we live
       & breaths, my friend, come easy

* * *

I dreamt of a *baita* high in my meadow's alp.
A moon on one side, on the other a mountain,
up above the angel of migration slowly rising
in her spiral trajectory towards the azures of
the night. Refugee who walked thousands of
miles to a non-arrival home. Journey of eight
days from high pastures to the market town.
Weeks of delay at the frontier and the death
of twin sons in sullen epidemics of measles.
Think of the mother's pain placing their tiny
and absent breaths in the palms of her hand.
I know it's a scarp slope vanishing into snow.
I know our macaronic earth shines in venom.
You glitter white we see you so from far off.
I know trench lines of war still sleep up there
above the charred poles and the thunder tree

toward the mountains that rise up in our sap.
I dreamed of a horse on the white sun slope.
This is not a dream that burns out with sleep.
This is a discourse I have with the physicists.
This is a dissonance where all our truths fail.
Sound is the music of radiant flutes pulsing
in us. My feet rise off the ground while they
remain on the floor, and, as vertical aphasias,
reel me back up high. Clarinets of the sun or
murmured silences give rhythm to my lungs.
I let the sound pass by above. This is it. My
friend, this is it.

* * *

I could tell you of the zones of coma cresting
beyond Lvov of the snows, or the Volga front.
Or you me rings of Saturn & their melancholy.
I could tell you of ice edges in the human soul
and you me about the old physics of serration.
The eyes of owls, swallows' flight & fish fins
and how all of these disinter our livid dreams.
I will tell you and you tell me over some beer
how crests of disaster overhaul us all or how
from the comas of sleep exerted form rises up
and gives us back our breath – just at the time
where we should stop breathing & cease to be.
Do we forget so easily cities that fell into seas
or how mountains of blood exploded, how so
many people in all centuries are made refugee.
Look at the angel of refugees and of migration.

Strange that this word 'cleansing' should have
a part in brutality. Strange that cogent beauty
in sciences we have come so to love & fail at
should brink us on the cusp of this disaster or
take us to our homes amid such homelessness.
Once more this music pulses radiance into us.
This is the incipient turn of the world into its
new millennium & half the world is flocking
to immure ourselves in distant magmas. No.
Clean song. Or angel light that clarifies in
turbid farce ...

They Came In ...

They came in a host of black coracles on
          the lookout for errant weed
They rock-perched like seabirds at the western
          extremities
They were erudite & ordinary, as all of us on
          this earth can be
They lived in small buildings where they could
          hear the yelping of gulls
They flew – and their thoughts – in apostolic
 migrations across the congested zones : –
          white cities blinking in the sun

They travelled in gulped mouths before ever
          they'd sit down to write –
and even then, like Fernando Pessoa, they'd
stand at their lecterns to write their books.
Their students would construct dictionaries
   of gone languages while supporting
          vast families.
Nothing unusual in shriving their skulls white
     while wearing back-packs & craving
          sackfuls of books.

Such was their sense of the beauty of speech !

They walked vast distances, their heads full with
          grammar & swallowed geographies.
They knew the skies by the lands they walked on.
Those who numbered the most solitary minds
          ever known in the west.

They drank heather honeys & organic blonde !

Everything comes down to the undertaking of
extravagant research on the lips of the
incoming tides ...

Siberian Pieces

Ancient

(suffering having driven the old man out of his wits,
and me to an insane pursuit of premature sanity :
Joginder Paul)

During the archaeological expeditions conducted under my guidance
in the years 1953 – 1957 for the State Historical Museum For Material
Culture, a large number of finds were exposed from the basins of the
Tomi and Yai rivers. These sites dated in the main from the neolithic
period and into the Bronze Age.

A statuette of a bear carved in sandstone was found in the Samus
burial ground. Its snout sculpted in a most realistic way, its lips,
nostrils and sharply curved forehead outlined and its eyes pointed
by some sharp object. The ears are in relief, the front paws shaped
in the form of small cylinders. The trunk is elongated and as if it could
be held by human hands, to carry or perhaps to present the bear.
The sandstone is rough, the sculpture a thing of beauty. Other tombs
contained burnt clay objects, a fish with transverse grooves on its
head, bone figures representing birds in flight, a necklace composed
of the teeth of wild animals and plates made of bone and stone.
Elsewhere nearby there was a bear's head carved from fine sandstone
and a human face chopped from the forehead and in addition stylised
human figures were found painted on vessels.

What the significance of these figures and representations is – indeed
whether there is any particular 'significance' we can know – perhaps
does not matter. As someone once said : there is still much to be done
in these fields. One thing, however is fairly certain : all these works of

art are proof of the rich spiritual content of the life of the inhabitants of the Tomsk region in these times. Why is it we find it so hard to think about such shadows of our forgotten ancestors, or assume that we in our lives have come to any better or deeper understanding of our lives or our earths ?

Diószegi 1

The Hungarian scholar Vilmos Diószegi was born in Budapest in 1923.

Born into a working-class family, which I mention only for accuracy, following secondary school he studied Tungus with Altaic & Mongolian languages in the Central Asian Studies Faculty at the University of Budapest. This staked out his way and journey through the remaining thirty years of his life : and he was lucky enough to have had an independent teacher in (Lajos Ligeti) and to have chosen a field of study sufficiently related to Hungarian history without being too close to its bone. I do not mean by this to suggest that he either felt at ease with the soviet bureaucracy of post-war Hungary, nor that he himself had a calm life under that system and regime. However he was able up to a point to carve out an area of research that matched his passion and suited the purpose of 'free' research. He was able to establish very good working relations with a number of Soviet ethnographers in Moscow and he was able to visit Siberia on three occasions for protracted field research – though the last occasion cut short further visits because he went beyond the limits of acceptability in the eyes of the academic bureaucrats and the security forces, travelling carelessly to distant and off-site villages and recording fragments of narrative and music without the least nod toward permission. He must in those years increasingly have tried the patience of those bureaucracies : and in turn his patience must often have been tried by them and in the end his health seriously undermined.

He died in 1971 at the height of his scholarly powers and with many books and theses unfinished. He died suddenly six months through a long and debilitating illness which had struck him down in September 1970 and in a sense he had never fully recovered from the rigours – both physical and political – of his last visit to Siberia in 1959. Had he been alive still in the year that I'm writing this he would only have been eighty-two, and the loss to all scholarship is hard to estimate.

What he left unfinished was an archive behind the eyes of time.

Diószegi 2

In one of his longer essays Diószegi relates the following :

'Shaman Kokuev told me how he had become a shaman : "I too was ill when that happened. First my head began to ache, then my hands. My head still does hurt when the moon is full. I was often visited by spirits and then when I was asleep my tongue sang. It sang as the shaman sings. But I knew nothing of this. When I woke up, my mother, my father and my sister all told me "You sang songs, you sang shaman songs". A few days later I would begin to feel better. But three or four months on it would begin over again. My head kept hurting again all the time and when I slept my tongue sang shaman songs. This kept repeating itself every few months for three years. You keep on suffering – suffering and suffering and when you want to rest or to sleep, then your tongue starts to sing. You can't do anything about it. Of course, you don't know these songs since they are sung by the spirit. But not all spirits sing in the same way. Some sing with beauty, some singing is ugly. The 'great spirits' sing best. I was twenty-seven when I first heard the spirit sing. I was visited by a 'little one'. It flew into my mouth and then I began to sing shaman songs. Later when I no longer had the strength to keep on suffering, I did what the spirit told me to do and I agreed to become a shaman. I changed completely after that, for a shaman turns you into an entirely different sort of person. So I became a shaman."'

The long winter following this, the shaman followed his dead mother across thin ice. Behind him hills shaped like triangles ululated on the horizon, as if they were just floating on his mind, as if they were forming a picture series, as if words had never been separated out from images in his pneuma, as if they were starting a narrative. According to unanimous opinion he had passed over into the world of his mother : but he must have come back again from time to time to sing her songs. Then such singing drives you into, not out of, your wits.

Love is concerned that the beating of your heart should harm no-one.

Friar Julian

The Dominican brother Friar Julian, during the reign of King Andrew II of Hungary and not long before the Mongol invasions of the first half of the 13th century, left his order-house and homeland with three other Dominican brothers with the intention of travelling eastwards to the Volga regions in search of those Magyar tribes left behind centuries earlier in their beyond-eastern homes. After a long and clearly dangerous journey he arrived alone in a region close by the Volga where he judged from the seeming familiarity of the language he heard spoken that he had come to where he had intended.

Returning to Hungary towards the end of 1236 he is said to have submitted a report to Rome, before setting out once more the following year to fulfil his journeys and expectations. This however was not to come to fruition since he heard from reports fast fleeing westwards that the advancing Mongols – hordes is a word I don't want to use, since I feel it differentiates us in our minds from people we are in effect the same as and inculcates an unfortunate sense of otherness in our perceptions – had overrun the regions he had been planning to return to. Once back in Hungary he never afterwards returned to the Volga or indeed journeyed eastward from the order-house at all. A description of his first journey was known from a report sent to Pope Gregory IX by the Dominican Friar Richard in a copy from a Vatican codex dating back to the last years of the 13th century. However even this copy seems to have disappeared, for what reason we can only conjecture, so that all we have to go on are generalised reports of Friar Julian's journeyings and hopes. On the puszta plains – not unlike the extensive fields of the Volga shoreline – he is said in his last years to have tended Dominican horses, until each spring he saw in the melting of ice and snow and the rising of orange suns through the translucent bellies of the mares and their sac-swum foals, familiar to him in their ways through his years of late shepherding, not so much evidence of the greatness of the Lord Creator as sharp song-thrusts from the origins of language and music. So at least it seemed to him, and who are we to doubt his vision.

Horse Island

On the island of horses sea pinks and tiny white daisies cover the shoreline on sand meadows above bright banners of seaweed. The horses wander these meadows cropping easily on the flowers and the strands of weed : it is good for their bones, it is good on the tongue.

There is no tension here, no need for dope or unctions or the remedies of shaman : it is the place that shaman come to themselves for deliverance. It is the paradise of time. When the walking over inlets of ice, when tramping slowly along the sheep paths and lakes in search of kindling, when the drinking of stewed teas and remedies, when these things are done, then suddenly it is the paradise of time. Horses graze spring meadows flecked with tiny flowers, sand and soil rise just above the sea-level, the sun is an orange orb through the translucent bellies of the pregnant mares, the days of ice are gone, the days of ash and fire also. This is not a dream, this is a repeated ploy of history, this is what is given & this is what is taken ...

Interim 1

Of the twenty-eight scholars who contributed to the compilation 'Popular Beliefs and Folklore Tradition In Siberia', which was edited by V. Diószegi and published first by Indiana University in Bloomington and by Mouton & Co. in The Hague in 1968, none are any longer alive. Even at the time of publishing – and much of the research reflected in the book's articles went back over the preceding forty years – even at that time five of the authors were no longer alive : namely W. Steinitz, G.D. Verbov, A.A. Popov, N.P. Dyrenkova and I. Paulson. Strangely all these scholars had contributed among the shortest articles, but that most surely can only be pure coincidence. Of the remaining twenty-three, twenty-two had died by the time of the book's next edition in London in 1997 and the remaining scholar, V.I. Matjuscenko – author of the brief but illustrated article on the 'Art of the Ancient Tribes of the Lower Tomi' cited above – died at the advanced age of ninety just after the turn of the century in the year 2000 in his native city of Tomsk.

Before giving some consideration to Matjuscenko's life – and it seems likely from his patronymic that his family had at some date migrated from the Ukraine – it is worth briefly looking at the end of the lives of a few of the other twenty-two scholars :

(...)

As to the life of V[ladimir] I[lych] Matjuscenko the first thing to note is that his parents had given him the forenames of the revolutionary founder of the Soviet state at a time when the latter was not widely known outside revolutionary circles of the far left or beyond the security forces of the old regime. We might assume therefore with some degree of certainty that the scholar's parents were either in sympathy with or even knew and worked with Vladimir Ilych Lenin and that in all likelihood they had been exiled to the region around Tomsk shortly after the 1905 revolution. V.I. Matjuscenko himself was born in January of the year 1910 in the city of Tomsk and died there in the first days of the year 2000. But of his life in the years between, we can at times only postulate an (............)

Kouchak

Nahapet Kouchak, about whom we know very little other than that he was a superb and very individual poet, was born or at any rate lived some time in the thirteenth or possibly the fourteenth centuries. Yegishe Charents wrote of him and Valeriy Bryusov pointed out in 1916 that he should not be identified with Nahapet Kouchak from the village of Kharakonis near Van who lived in the 1500s. He is reputed to have been a gardener and he may well have been. He was, for sure, a lunatic of the god of love and perfection, he was what in other words we have often needed from a poet. No doubt he walked out of his room and saw vivid blue hanging over the courtyard and a little further off white mountains suspended as a constant miracle behind his village. No doubt he knew that if we talk only to the buildings & people on the village streets, there is little point in our breathing, but that if we also talk to & of the mountains that rise up behind the streets, if we talk to both, then perhaps it has been worth our being alive. Giacometti, we might suggest, thought much the same. He knew that even if he worked at a portrait for a thousand years he would only, and that with luck, approach a little closer to his intentions. Just as he knew it is precisely at the moment we realise that nothing is possible & admit to the necessity of giving up, it is only and precisely then that we might succeed just slightly in achieving our aims. Possibly he, that is to say Nahapet Kouchak, put his manuscripts out on the rooves to dry when weak sunlight emerged after the ecstatic downpours, though this act is more usually attributed to Sayat Nova in the 1700s. But let us presume that they both did this and that Giacometti looked on, between painting his mother and sculpting his wife, between scratching away at his brother and fucking his mistress, with something like approval. I happen to have a small book of Kouchag's poetry, unfortunately only in English translation apart from the title page and its colophon. Unfortunately, not because of the quality of the translations – which are by Ewald Osers and are very good – but rather simply because the (pneumas)* of the Armenian don't face them. This book though is like one of those paper flowers that – scrunched tight – opens out completely when it's placed in water. When Kouchag lived, when and how he died, we don't know, but what we do know is that if we hang his words out to dry after superb rains we will be rewarded with the incomparable harvest of translation. Try telling that to one of the bureaucrats who rule away and fiddle about with our words and our lives and give us the lie.

*Osip Mandelstam's description of the Armenian language ...

Mészáros

The Hungarian artist Lászlo Mészáros was arrested in 1938 in Siberia
– where he had chosen to go and live with his family after 1932 – and
presumably was executed in the same year. A not unusual fate : we
might think also of Osip Mandelstam, or the less well-known Estonian
poet Heiti Talvik, as of course of many others. Lászlo Mészáros met
his fate though, because – apart from being a fine artist – he was an
unreconstructed Marxist, or rather because he was a communalist
of the oldest pre-Leninist school, and as such, through his passionate
belief in community, clashed with a regime that from its very outset
betrayed in the most abject fashion the community it grew out of.
How could such a human being have survived through those days
and years : not possible, not in any way possible.

Mészáros was born in September 1905 – the same year as József Attila
– in Kobanya, a poor working-class town such as József might have
known. Such sectors both no longer exist : and yet also still very
much exist in totally unchanged and totally changed states. His
father had worked as a foundryman in the steel mill of Csepel Island,
a stronghold of radical workers' movements. He went voluntarily to
Siberia in 1931, the same year his daughter was born, taken there by
inspired conviction. Without doubt he felt that his life and his work
were stretched out before him and when he was arrested in the year of
our Stalin 1938 he thought it was a mistake and laughed – his daughter
always remembered this – because he reckoned he would be heading
back home very soon, back to the summer sun, back to his sculpture.

His daughter Mártá – born in Budapest but removed to Soviet Central
Asia in the year of her birth – grew up to become one of the foremost
Hungarian film-makers. In 1978 she made a film 'In Memoriam : Lászlo
Mészáros' and from 1982 onward produced the trilogy 'Diary For
My Children'(1982), 'Diary For My Loves'(1987) and 'Diary For My

Father And Mother'(1990). This almost goes without saying, as does the difficulty she has faced finding funding for her more important and risky films of the late 1990s. But of the films concerning her father, much much more needs to be said.

And of her father she has written 'His art died in 1938 when they took him away. I do not remember much of him ... if we do not preserve his memory, his life and art will become part of our forgotten past.' Or are our own lives just the shadows of forgotten ancestors ? Does the sun only shine through the belly of a spring-starved horse ? Doesn't the foetus of energy pulse there in its egg-swum sac ?

Little father, what is the point of these histories or of the soups of memory into which are dipped our prison spoons ?

Nur Baba

'Nur Bâbâ was a mullah in the Yaghnab Valley in north-western Tadjikistan. A very remote place and with only a horse track across the pass that led into and out of it : nonetheless, or perhaps not surprisingly, it also was highly cultured and not a few children from the valley grew to become scribes or teachers or poets. Because of its remoteness the valley began to come under Soviet influence and control only in the mid-1920s and in fact remained much its own place until the 1950s when villages were emptied and the inhabitants transplanted wholesale to the recently established cotton-growing collective in the flatlands of Z. Then for twenty years and despite attempts by some villagers to return to Yaghnab, the valley remained almost wholly without inhabitants until 1981 or so, when a few old villagers with some of their families were able to move back relatively unimpeded. By the 1990s most villages, including some of the most remote, had at least one or two families. Nur Bâbâ's was one of these. His daughter had married but remained childless, and she had lost her memory from various beatings suffered at the hands of the Security Forces in Z and from the sadistic murder of her husband at the same hands. Nur Bâbâ's father and grandfather, both mullahs, had studied in a *madrasah* in Bukhara, but this had been shut down by the time it was his turn to study and therefore he had been educated in secrecy and at home. In the mid-1920s – when Soviet authority had penetrated Yaghnab – his father had put his religious books and texts into a sealed box and sent them floating down the fast-flowing Yaghnab river. We can only imagine the bitter flux of despair and faith and sanctioned madness that had allowed him to do this, but perhaps we can well imagine. The township they had lived in for centuries – and to which the family returned in 1983 – was known as Piskân which name approximates in meaning to "hidden source of knowledge". By some miracle of the power of pure rage or from some sufic sagacity, the sealed box with texts intact was saved by a turtle that had, apparently, pushed it up onto warm sands with its snout from the wild rushes it had become snagged up in a day's journey downriver.'

Shaman

In the early spring following his mother's death, the shaman walked out behind the shadow of his mother beneath the foot of the mountains across thin ice. Some of his comrades walked on the edges behind him. In the middle of the inlet the shadow of his mother turned round and gave him the warmth of her smile before dissolving off in the ice haar. The shaman continued walking until he reached the far shore of the sound, to a place he had not visited in twenty years. There in the hut made of joined fir logs, where once he had been mesmerised by the illusions of a premature sanity, were the remnants of his bedding and his studies and his last meal. Staying there a week in honour of his mother, he then returned across the ice and its screen of wind-shovelled sleet pellets to the village of his brothers and sisters where he wrote the text that has come down to us as 'the discourse on the sanities' or else as 'unified string theory'. It bears an uncanny resemblance to the medieval Persian text known as 'String Beads of the (............)' but cannot in any way be thought to be derivative of it, nor is there any evidence, or reason, to suppose that the shaman knew of the Persian text.

Years later – as if in another life and buoyed by the red sulphurs of the sun – the shaman stood at the edge of a warmer sea : from beneath a headland with a white castle a crowd of women in black cloaks climbed into a large row-boat and set off across the sea for a visible shore. And as the boat veered in a curve away from the shore, the stragglers went calf-deep into the sea to wave the travellers away ...

Where does language come from ? From where have we managed to enact it ? And what is the string of continuity in our insane pursuit of premature exactitude ?

Love is to know when not to follow the patterns of string, the juices of fruit, the tangents of compassion that mesmerise all of us.

Urgunge Onon

The Mongolian scholar Urgunge Onon who lived most of his academic life first in America and then in England, was in fact born – on the eleventh day of the eleventh lunar month of 1919, corresponding to the lunar date 1 January 1920 – in a village in north-eastern Inner

Mongolia. His family hunted and farmed in a remote area close by
the Manchurian border and had retained a dialect (Daur) long lost
by the majority of Mongols. During his youth he enjoyed traditional
Mongolian pursuits wrestling, horse riding and hunting and also
managed to acquire an understanding of shamanic rituals that were
still practiced at the time. A sense of the importance of shamanism
remained with him throughout his life. Whilst still young he was
held hostage by bandits and suffered from the endemic warring of
the time. From the time of the Communist takeover and then for the
rest of his days long journeyings become a way of life for him, as if
the logical outlines of his 'career' were fed by an inner adherence to
the philosophies of shamanism. If the journeys he made on horseback
were relatively short, he nonetheless felt that, as with his ancestors
in the thirteenth century, vertiginous journeys and migrations across
continents had become a way of life for him.

At different times in his life he worked as a middle-school teacher and
bodyguard for the Inner Mongolian prince Demchügdongrob (also
known as De Wang), met and befriended the scholar Owen Lattimore,
worked in US universities, lost jobs because of McCarthyite
intrigues, started a Mongolian Studies Programme at Leeds
University (in 1968) and helped establish the Mongolia and Inner
Asia Studies Unit at Cambridge (in 1986). His knowledge of the
archaic Daur dialect enabled him to analyse hidden textual problems
in the 'Secret History Of The Mongols'. In 1966 he made his first trip
back to Mongolia since leaving in 19[..] and was presented with a
horse and saddle on visiting the river Onon locale of his family home.

*I have taken these details largely (and freely) from the brief biography
of his father contributed by Temujin Onon at the opening of the volume
of the journal 'Inner Asia' (Vol. 2, No. 1, 2000) celebrating the eightieth
birthday of Urgunge Onon. What I have added would hardly fill an
ellipsis (............).*

Four Essays

Algebra & Poetry

There is the principle that the sum of the whole is greater than the parts.

Thus in a wall in which there appears to be no door or entrance, there may be a door. Thus every history in fact has a possibility, even if only a limited choice of 'actual histories' may in fact have occured.

Thus translation is possible even in the most difficult of circumstances.

The algebra of the world is expressed in its poetic structure.

Algebra is the music of poetry. And it is pain & salvation in the world.

I mean the above in the sense of mathematical lemmas ...

Poetry is a concatenation of its various components : it is more than just one element and it is greater than the sum of its parts. Poetry opens up in language – in the ways we say things – what appeared not to be there before, as well as giving linguistic expression to what we already might have felt or known.

Poetry is more than the sum of its parts : in this respect it has the same mapping as does algebra, or any system of mathematical lemmas.

Algebra/al-gebr/al-jabr : the science of restoring what is missing and equating like with like. The science of the reduction of what has been fractured so as to retain within it some form of integrity, which is to say structural/mathematical wholeness.

Al-jabr : from the Arabic & from the scholarship of Arabic treatises.

Poetry : a system of representing or expressing spiritual structures in terms of language.

Poetry : the creation or relevation of a gap/hole in a surface/wall where such a gap was not previously thought to exist.

Poetry : the most effective method of progressing from point 'a' to point 'b' that both succinctly expresses the relation between 'a' & 'b' and that also most richly relates the context of the wider universe where points 'a' & 'b' exist.

That experience where two elements melt together & then separate out again.

I would like to say that poetry is the sun of its parts (sic : 'sun')

A Few Notes On Flat Plate Theory

The flight of some birds : swift and precise.

I do not know the mathematical symbols or equations of this.

The stylised shape of the bird's body and beak : fast (rapid) and exact.

This is the nature of mathematical equata and lemmas : precise and fast.

But take the model of bird-flight and the shapes of the bird's body as it flies. Think of a cormorant or a gannet, and then try to envisage the complex simplicity of the mathematical formulae that might define and describe this : impossible !

And yet what I am wanting to say and reach is precisely that !

The notion that within many naturally occurring phenomena (but what does this mean ?) there are present a range of flat plates and planes : and then to envisage functions of these plates and planes and the exact description of the variations implicit within such functions ...

As perfect as a cormorant flying toward the sun ! Or as a gannet-plunge ...

The aerodynamics, (the marine dynamic !), the unique physics, the metaphysics, the exact equation and formula of one gannet plunging after a fish !

Just as Leoš Janáček, wherever he went, would write down snatches of speech for their melodies : meticulous in pitch, rhythm, phrase length, time and timing.

There are an infinite number of models and expressions within the universe or in any one small part of the universe. To whorl down from such infinity onto precise examples and functions of such models : and then spiral out again to the infinite.

It is this : to focus on the flatness of a plate or plane and then to envisage the spiral out from this function, as exactly and precisely as a gannet's plunge.

The flatness of a static plane arrow-signs the function of the spiral.

Then to realise that the function of a spiral/whirl/whorl is not only a model of action or enactment, but that it is a physical reality in and of itself.

Take the model of a bird's 'precision & speed' : and then functionally elaborate.

Poetry is a gannet-plunge into the sea for sustenance, it is the cormorant flying at the sun in the search for light and precise breath !

On Hesitancy

Conversations with Sheila Beskine :

The accumulation of slow accreted insights or processes of
understanding.

The sense that some insights or indeed attributes may be swift, sharp,
exact : but that others of equal validity may be slow, built up, not
immediately apparent.

The power of action and ambition may bias insights that are fast
and logical.

The clear way to reach a point in front of you is to go directly towards
it : a richer way may though be to describe a circle that at first seems
to move away from that point, only to reach it later in the circle's
(the curve's) completed arc.

Is the universe only compounded of straight lines or of curves and
curved planes ?

Sheila's point is that in understanding oneself and in understanding
other people, a statement of sharp and clear perception may of itself
block off those other, equally valid processes that are accretional and
slowly apparent.

It may well be that many people in fact process slowly and in hidden
ways.

Therefore it is very important to understand and also to accommodate
such slow processes and the principle of slowness, of hiddenness.

Let's say that there is something implicitly beautiful about being
hesitant.

Let's at least say that there may well be something of beauty in being
hesitant.

Narrative also is non-linear and likely it is the richer for being so.

'A Hundred Years Of Solitude' is not a linear forwards progression :
much more it is a circular movement that begins by shifting backwards.

Many narratives resist linearity and reach their completion by
sideways shifts. This would seem to be true within fiction and with
our lives.

Much within politics, or the politics of ambition and power, and
within commerce is compelled by linear logic, is empowered by
progression.

(A phrase here that JJ said apropos of other things : but I may not
remember it)

Some Thoughts On A Physics of Poetry

Poetry is akin to energy and breath.

Poetry is the breath of energy, it is energy and breath together.

In this, poetry is related to physics, both are marked by energy. Poetry is not so much to do with language – a 'fault' of the 'language poets' – as with physics.

Poetry is the mathematics of flowers. By which I mean that poetry has to do with structure and with structures in the world.

Poetry is a mathematics of flowers : all three share the existence of structures in the world, structures that have been in existence for many millions of years.

It is very difficult to eradicate all traces of the structure of the world. Similarly it is very difficult to eradicate all sense of poetry from the world.

The intent of commercial logic – which is to destroy the structure of the world and, as if by accident, the need for poetry *inter alia* – is in fact a narrow, imperfect aim.

A tree is a *bomb* of breath. That is, it explodes life slowly around itself. It gives life. It is therefore not true that all bombs are destructive.

Explosions may be slow or fast, which anyway are relative terms. Life on earth has been exploding very slowly over the course of thousands of millions of years.

The patterns planted into and extracted from the earth by its forms of life are so complex and so resilient and also so beautiful and mathematically precise that it would be almost impossible to totally destroy them.

Poetry is therefore a mathematics of flowers, or of bird-flight.

Patterns are printed and planted exactly.

Stepney Poem

I.

Between St. Katherine's
& the new circle of Limehouse Basin
the thick storeys of John Scurr House

built like a multilevel car park
but with crushed flats in place of vehicles
in days when cars were still scant

                    *

John Dart grew up there
to play skiving & pool. To play word games
because truly they were great philosophers
in John Scurr House

John drank in the Nelson & drinks
now in the Five Bells or Queen's Head. I like
the rough blade-bone of his language : it's

true and lies and fences. It is exact
to what he needs & pots the colours of his
meanings exactly right.

It is for him to always laugh at his
                    failures.

                    *

As to who John Scurr was
I don't know. Or rather, I do. Some real
socialist of the 1920s & the Rent Riots.
Or I don't know – John Dart I do – but I'll
find out before this poem's ended.

2.

Down at the canal with fishing men
& graffiti & bottles & trash & summer
I look for poetry. Don't let me find it
from the fisher king who's an illusion.
Among condoms & discarded syringes
I watch the slow graceful flight of
          a mid-morning heron

And know the shit it causes for these
enterprise zones, letting fall what it likes
& its slow wing-beats passing.

                    *

Shall we stop at Bill Mayes' for a mug
of tea & one of his slabs of jam slice.
The air of the road is cruel. I
shall stop at Bill Mayes' for a mug, an
eyeful of light from the resident cat.

Shall I go to the backwoods depths of
Limehouse Library past Attlee's stone
(but he's been decanted into Q'Mary's
          to oversee the caterwaul café)

to ask Robert Walser to accompany me
on this slow twenty-hour marathon in
        the dusts of the mountains ?
Or Fernando Pessoa, but that someone
from Fieldgate Mansions has already
        bagged his serene company.
John, are we not alive in London now ?
Mario, Mario I fear the heron shrieks.
And who am I to disagree ? I'll not
        divulge anything.

3.

David Kessel doesn't live far from here.
I can tell him by short-crops of his hair.
He stayed in a tower block that's since
been pulled down to make way for some
six-laner highway that beheaded his lair.
Or no, he was once a doctor in Poplar.
I know it's true, you need to believe me.
We can go & see him in his kestrel's air.
(I'm saying all this to my friend Robert
        Walser, you understand)
That is, up six flights of stairs in Roche
House, up Gill Street past the Health &
Safety Centre where he takes in those
        roofless in mind & body.

                    *

(One time he told me I should become
vagrant on the streets if I was really a

poet. And he was right I now reflect as
I manoeuvre the stiff dusts of this hill.)

*

All roads lead back to John Scurr House.
Except that it has been emptied now of its
people for the sake of Limehouse Village.
Or for the sake of some Silk District or a
similarly misnomered life disaster zone.

4.

Nonetheless, all roads do lead back to John
          Scurr House. Here. Now.
I myself am walking back that way & as I go
I see glide past me in a silence of torn nerves
John Dart & his dear old mother & his son
(& all the wishing she never did is still there
          in the skies)
& Nazrul Islam with books piled in his arms
(in the days before fire burnt his libraries &
thugs attacked him up Bromley-by-Bow &
made him fear to walk out in his own town).

In the days before he died in Sylhet Town.

& David Kessel carrying a mountain on his
          back
Bill Mayes filling Limehouse Basin all those
          years with tea so folk could drink &
David Silver mumbling to the epileptic God

Miranda Kellas in a tiny plane with her son
Ralphie (look how they wheel in & out of
          all the furtive traffic)
Will James at the helm of his great & ship-
    wrecked hull (Hi Will!)
he who gave up doctoring for art & then he
          gave up art for doctoring again
(& even Wilma on her mountain bike : look
at the great bruise on her gashed knee), Ian
Orton – not Joe, he was never here, too far
to go – he who ran the crooked Council &
was at least warmed at my unkempt words
even though he'd to resign in the end & go.
          And then not least John Dart
who knew sufficiently of raw ruby courage
tempering life in an ordinary savage heart
among the various councillors & drinkers
& finally John Scurr himself leading a riot
gaffing it against all Poll Taxes & recalling
the hard words of unsweet matchstick girls
& I am there furling my little flag of words
among them all & I am here flagging my
          furl of words for all of us to hear.

5.

I saw Jock McFadyan up the Limehouse
          Cut : a pure sodium was
lighting up beneath its grey electric sky
& he was contemplating the patina of his
streets, how a horse might come to lament
the invention of the car. He painted Harry

Diamond dancing in a prefab in Stepney :
Harry dancing as he did twenty years later
in the George up down Commercial Road,
his feet twinkling, his body swayed awry :
alright, ok : it must be time to go anyway.

He painted Three Colts Lane as if it were
a horse got drunk on unnatural disasters.
He painted Turners Road as if it were a
rented studio where no rent was ever paid
& Will James & Dave Fried & Sue Brown
fileted manias against life's obscene grace
& artists partied until a drunk moon was
      dancing on their jaws.
Nazrul Naz lived just round the corner in
Clemence Road from where his life began
to fall apart & his libraries be drowned
               or burnt : a
little fire-puff of anarchy in London – two
streets & some few years gone from where
Astrid Proll had parsed incognito as a car
         mechanic & a good one too.
Jock McFadyan lived & painted there on
        Turners Road :
all his girls & graffiti, all the writing on
his walls, the girls waiting for the lads in
their cortinas, the lads waiting for better,
the doused patience of their parents, the
patina of those streets : the sodium wall
lighting up beneath its grey electric skies
& he was contemplating in his retina the
paths, how a horse might come to lament
the invention of the car, or a drunk man
      mistake a gantry for a bar.

* * *

All this is long-past now :
Dave Kessel lives in sheltered housing on
Arbour Square, Will James has two kids
& doctors as psychiatrist out in Southend
(but they live still in Stepney by the Kirk).
John Dart I've lost knowledge of, Nazrul's
back & forth to Sylhet – poet of Shadwell.
Miranda's decanted to Bristol many years
back. Ralphie flew there with her. Other
friends I've not mentioned in this poem.
Limehouse Basin's Limehouse Basin : no
more need be said. Robert Walser's left :
He's been confined to books ... It's 2015.
                    Or maybe it's 2025.
Shit ! I've had to eat so much of it. And
            now there's no time left ...

A Month Of Sundays / (Unruly Prose Poems)

* I

I am in a city.

There is a wooden house. It is coloured blue and red and green.
It is the length of four houses. It is like a little ship drunken in its
sea. It is floating off the pavement and the pavement itself is floating
in centuries of amnesia. I am walking past this house. I am walking
past all of this and I am swaying in my dream. The same city a few
days later : I've crossed a wooden bridge over the city's stream as if
going into a zone and session of old anarchists. The road rises up a
little and the whole street is dug up and being resurfaced & cobbled
(as was the street in Mala Strana the last time I was in Praha). I pass
the Užupis Bar though I'll go back there later, and walk upwards. A
line of houses, a few old men eating oranges, a tree I don't know &
a school that resembles a barracks and another wooden house of
many colours that is a hostel. I am slowly levitating but the whole
street and all the zone of damaged history is keeping pace with me.
This is the beginning and this is the end. I cannot say anything else :
all I can do is take the dream into my body as I walk. To know this
city at the pace of walking. To walk into Užupis as into a mirage.

It must have been Vilnius, this city, except it's no longer there.

This is all I can say.

There is a remoteness in the flagged floor.

Upstairs lived the young Hassidic scholar who never grew old, not
even when he was taken away by force to the electronic treatment camp.
Up there on the fourth silk-weaving floor in the room filled with books
and bread and beds. I never believed all the people who said he must have
led an insane life hemmed in with illness. For myself, I knew he walked
out like anyone else, that he ate in the cafés, that he always stopped and
gave his scant money to beggars, that he went to the baths and to the
string shop, that he lived life. How can I believe what so many people
say but is not true. And there is a remoteness in the flagged floor : as if
a book had been written on it and the last many pages were left unfilled
by intention. Or a registry of the shtetl when suddenly all births ceased.
The grey book, the meridian, the border crossing, the site of a little
subversion. Red sulphur rises up in a thought, crushes thought and
allows thought to rise and fly. What else can be said about his life ?
Not that it was that unusual. Or that what he held is a lesson to us ? Or
that ... The shop of string is shut-up and gone. They say a museum
of migration inhabits that space now, but I'm not sure about that.

* 3

And then in the circle of trees ...

* 4

And in the mountains ...

* 5

A great arc of houses, of tenements seen from beyond their yards.
A great arc. Nothing is as it seems, nothing is as it was. Lord bless us
for our nothing, Lord keep us in peace. Let us walk through this city,
we will bounce back from the stretched filaments and lining of lungs.
Where Gaon of Vilna, where Gaon Eliyyahu ben Shelomoh Zalman
lived and wrote his basics of algebra and geometry, not to mention his
astronomy and elements of Hebrew Grammar, and where he talked to
many thousands in the streets : now there is a wall and a small school
for young children. If you walk the tracery of alleys and narrow paths
you will be bounced through to a time of cinnamon streets & angels.
In one of the empty churches that was used as a war-time arms dump.
Beautiful are the churches of this city, beautiful their unrestored state,
beautiful the life of Gaon, beautiful the city in its signature of circles,
beautiful the singing lives of the children, beautiful. Lord bless us in
our Nothing. But Lord, why the sons of Gaon of Vilna slaughtered in
holocaust & then why their sons in their turn refusing the sanctuary
of home to Palestine ? Why they in their turn levelling the villages of
Palestinians in the abuse of the orange groves and almonds ... ?

* 6

On the rubble in front of the burning library, a cellist.
That life is the journey that we all make across breath.
That even the fence-posts of the sanatorium play music.
That their wire spikes are vestigial fingers to stroke hair.
That hair once stroked shall never be burnt or pillowed.
That hair is the most beautiful of journeys across breath.
That breath is the most beautiful of journeys across life.
To stroke is not to strike, the stricken always are struck.
That the blue beads around the neck are beads of love.

That hair spread over a pillow is the breath-span of love.
That music played through fire is an opening to heaven.
That a cello's belly is where babies of beauty are born.
A cellist on the rubble, in front of the burning library.

* 7

When the great scholar of red sulphur left the city of Cordoba
in the year 1201 new worlds opened up such as no-one imagined
and when the poet of divine filth danced out onto the Amber Sea
in the footsteps of Judah Halevi (or was it the other pursuing him ?)
the dolphin of poetry leapt through scorched stigmata of bruised air
When the great scholar of red sulphur did these things, the egg of
Garcia Lorca leapt in the womb of the world seven centuries later
& that whitened gully & drift of belched stone beckon us to vomit,
to vomit the exegesis of banned language, to vomit the stricken sky
of disappeared workers, to vomit the language of diseased politics,
to vomit the vomit we are forced to digest, o green of my green, o
dark magnolia of your belly, o persian horses dancing in the air,
o between gypsum & jasmine, o mouth of your death, Federico.

* 8

I am hanging on by a very thin thread.
In the last minutes of the second Friday of the first month of that
year, hooligans (those lovely exhausted sufi roisterers of poverty and
pain) invaded my empty house and stole the little word machine off
from my desk. The rest of the house defeated them filled with books
and papers and dust and clothes, dried vegetables, clotted yoghurts
and the discourses of Shams Tabrizi. Heroin addicts needing moneys

for the weekend fix they stole my little word machine and with it all the words I'd written down in my previous life. Did I thank them for freeing me of disorder and cohesion, something I'd not managed in thirty years of hard labour. Or did I go out raving and shrieking on the streets gull-mouthing my bereavement. Whatever, I left the next day for the mountains. A few words may have dribbled back to you about all this. I am hanging on by a very thin thread. Don't let me go, let me go, don't let me. Clotted yoghurts bubble around my rooms.

* 9

Every piece of language comes bursting, whole blocks of words
I vomit the whole contents of so many stomachs : this is what the
ocean is, this is the purity of hydrogen and oxygen, this is salt lesion
every piece of language comes bursting out : I vomit the contents
of so many stomachs, I vomit the vomit we're forced to inhale ...

* 10

Three years later to the minute, that explosion of anger.
That burning through the gauze of my nervous system until
only a blackened crust remained, until only a nerve remnant
danced on the laboratory bench, until only a few blue beads
are left and they surround the scorched tar of bone. What is
the wad of a banker compared to an old woman song-thrush !
Three years to the minute (second Friday of the first month
and just a handsel of moments before midnight) when you exploded your anger at the lost & stolen words. Beautiful this
world, beautiful our breathings on the crust of atomic rage.
Look at what the poet-philosopher – first great anarchist ! –

from Cordoba left in his travels through the Aleppo lands :
he who also donkeyed it toward Damascus as the white ship
set sail over the desert for the City of Homs & reason tried
to jump from barque to barque to reach the further shore
and white wolves surrounded the birth-house of logic and
half-gobbled raspberries were gobbled on nipples and the
child lost his father and the mother went insane and all of
our fig trees were scorched from their fields and we lived
in our blood vessels as if inside a breast and the blue of the
desert glistened with dark blood & the white ship of Reason
set sail to the City of Homs that never was close by the sea ...

* II

Language is a hedgehog under the hut, a red and green ...

* 12

In the backroom of a café five or six men talking round a table.
Yiddish probably. Beyond the rows of doughnuts and strudels
that form a sort of channel for them / a sort of light tunnel for
their passage. They resemble beggars and they resemble people
who always give to beggars whatever their means and it's scant.
One of the beggars says "it's against the law to beg" I say "what
is the law" as we all live together. In the backrooms of language
there where all of us have congregated for centuries. In the café
off the market with the widest pavements in the city. Opposite
the Hospital, since all of us fear we must go there at some time.
And years later I do go there but inside I make a painting with
many levels and surfaces and I write on the surfaces together

with poems and fragments in many languages (let's say Bangla, and Turkish and Somali and English and Urdu, let's say Nazrul and Oktay and Garriyye and Blake and Faiz, at the very least) I write into the painting 'translation is a vital art, words translated through the heart ...' then I walk out into the sunlight & indeed the sun's light is an unavoidable pleasure, indeed translation is a vital art, indeed I am happy to walk here with all my fellow beggars in a marvellous festival of beggary.

* 13

A new arts centre by the river : water curving away and a full moon that splashes. My friend Ivan, my friend Raquel, my friend Roy, my friend Dominic, my friend Caroline, my friend Carlota, my friend Daniele, my friend Theo, my friends Ziba and Amir, my friend Sarah, my friend David, my son Miqesh, my daughter Anna. On the way back east on the underground we laugh and collapse. And at Whitechapel a young woman gets on, offers us some cake, she works in the Café off the Lane, she knows us from Sundays and poetry, she knows us from milk and roses, she knows we have come from many places, all of us to be together here on this train, despite the collectors of tickets, the utterers of recorded nonsense, she knows why we are talking and therefore she offers us cake ... She offers us cake and we take it, we break it up and we pass it round and we examine it in our own ways and we toss it away into our mouths and we eat it and we devour it and then we are happy. And we go off each to our homes, the one at the top of the high-rise and the other too, the one to his nomadic madness and the other to her premature sanity, the one to Cuba and the other to Wapping, and which is the further none of us are sure, the one to his nipple and the other to her cunt, the one to his dope and the other to her death, and all of us are alone and all of us are together and all of us quite simply all of us, very probably all of us, and for sure ...

* 14

(Shirin Neshat : her film)

The coast near Tarifa where the Mediterranean and the Atlantic
Ocean join. White beaches favoured by the sufis of southern Spain
as places of meditation. On a headland a castle of tyranny & from
the sands below where ancient schists curl their cool a boat rowed
only by women and carrying only women sets out across the strait.
The last woman to board jumps on the gunnel-rail leaving behind
at the waves-break a crew of burkha-ed sisters and the boat curves
away toward white and distant cliffs. In the castle redundant men
wait and listen. In the boat and on shore women with words painted
on their lips, their eyelids, their foreheads, their breasts, their navels,
their thighs and inner thighs, their hands and their feet. In Persian,
as their sister Forrugh Farrokzhad might have said : 'all poetry is
rhymed with shit'. On another island of the western Mediterranean
and in another city, their brother Ramon Llull awaits them with his
plunder of eyelids and archives of air. What is meditation if not the
struggle for physical survival heightened to infinity. What is a sun's
white light if not unappeasable difficulty and absolute compassion.
White beaches and bays and the dreams of black-cloaked women
turned to stone and resting before the onslaughts of dry tides ...

* 15

(Pirosmani : his life)

As a path crests a hill there is a shop.

He gives away bread and oil to the un-moneyed poor.
To the emissary of the princes he sells loaves and vessels

of oil. Round cheeses and olives and yoghurt. On the walls
of the taverns of the city in the mountains he puts paintings.
Of a giraffe. A most beautiful one, a very real one. Between
such walls of brown rock he learns what it is to be human &
he sleeps in a broom cupboard against the snow ruts of the
winter. He gives good bread away to the un-moneyed poor.
Aniseed loaves he has hung up to dry along the rafters. Up
in the mountains they've built a railway to bring him fame.
In the taverns he has two jugs full of red wine and he drinks.
His friends desert him. They think he has died because no-one
has seen him in months. In fact he is asleep in his abandoned
shop. Life is very slow around him – the birds sing slowly,
the brown rock hardly moves, the wooden town-houses
graze like placid cows in thick abundant grass. Peasants
stamped through the previous century's snow to his shop.
On the walls his paintings gleamed and flickered ...

* 16

Words on the lips. Words painted on the lips. Painted
on the lips of a woman in Persian. Words of a poem. A
poem by Forrugh Farukhzad. Words painted along the
lips, painted by a woman along her own labia ...

* 17

A bird, I cock my head into the darkness.
This is a dream, this is only a dream. But only dreaming
keeps us alive, only dreams keep us rooted and grounded.
To what is real. Keep us from the deluge of deluded logic.

Only insanity keeps us from the realisation of premature
derision. A bird, I cock my head into the darkness, I dip
my beak into colour, I paint with my wings onto cloud,
I break all the laws of geometry with my body's flight,
I dance with my body to the clarinets of the sun.
This is a dream, this is only a dream.

* 18

Moses Maimonides walked down Cable Street.
Well he did, didn't he : you can't go trying to no-say me.
Moses Maimonides arm in arm with my friend Ibn Arabi.
The streets were dark that night, the curlicues were falling
off the old shop-fronts. Tower blocks were lit with pastel
shades and late on in the night they'd get up and walk out
to the suburbs. Schoolkids with their teachers were off to
look for mushrooms in the tight melancholy of fox-days.
If I said yes, I'd mean no : if I said no, I'd mean nothing.
Sirens roosted on the roof-tops of newly done-up flats. A
pillow book from Mulberry Girls fell out onto the tarmac.
What I tried to do I couldn't, what I didn't try worked to
perfection : well it would wouldn't it. It's how things are.
Polystyrene into cardboard, spineker unto boats of reeds,
Drugs' needles on kids' playground grass, swimming pool.
Moses Maimonides walking down Cable Street : arm in
arm with my friend Ibn Arabi : and the marvel is both of
them have left two poems graffitied to the market wall.

* 19

I am out on the moor.

Dead gulls are blown on the storm winds. The lake speaks.
Ice walks like footsteps along the lake's edge. The island
that was a haven of endangered language. The island that –
as the boat moved away from it – itself seemed to be sailing
into its own extinct sun where seabirds blister & blacken.

I am out on the coma crests of that moorland.

* 20

I am out on the ledge.

I am standing there on my uppers. Under the blue.
Then I kick out and I am flying. This is how it will have to be.
This is the beginning and the end. The ease of life has caved in.
This is the open definition of freedom. This is the absence of
All constriction. This is the tricky numbness of dizzied height.
This is where the inner stairwell collapses in on the sane self.
This is the beginning of ending. This is the start of calm zero.
These are blue beads of time defying all translation : this
Is the edge of the world and this is its wonder & beauty.

5 Pebbles From the Shore And One Other

sandstone you
red and brown veined
from the cliffs of Angus or
so far north we'd forget
space and love

beautiful heart,
lozenge, perfect kidney,
sluice of my breathing
sieve of my sanity

        *

pink marble
pebble with traces of
garnet and bruised blood

what spasms of plankton
buffetted you into the wedge
into the face-shape with veins
you are showing me now

        *

tiny spade of
white, quartzite veined
with astonishing green, and
speckled along your fire zone
with red flecks

what traumas
you have gone through
I have gone through too

       *

gneiss or
mica schist glinting in
the fire-winds of your silence :
green and black your heat
that quenches and does
not burn

the metamorphoses
by fire and magma that
pulse-crushed you to beauty :

I know that – I know – I know
that the crystals knitted to fusion
are deep dug inside me too

       *

rune stone
sediments crushed by layer
until you resemble white writing

something told me
millions of years ago about
the bruising in your blood

but only now, now
on the shore of this North Sea
can I read what you are
saying

*

little milk-pill
with a brown burn mark
little blue bead, you are

what is translated
by time

I will put you
round my neck
a stringed pendant

I will swallow you
since everything that is
swallowed is like lava

like fire that quenches
and does not burn

saliva of life

Aldeburgh/Whitechapel November 2001/January 2002

IX.

Birds of East London

Máirtín Ó Direáin

Máirtín, I walked to your home
from the ferry pier at Cill Rónáin : it
was a lovely five miles, though it took me
fifty years. But it was a beautiful walking,
wild garlic on your paths, cormorant seas,
honeysuckle, furling bracken, honey bees.
I blew you a kiss when I got to your house
though you might not have wanted a kiss.
The little stream shimmied down the shore.
Below your barn bare limestone then more,
your stone path with tiny lilies going down.
A rain cloud is gathered across the spine of
your island where the houses climb the hill
above Corrúch where I walked into silence
and spoke with horses and lay down asleep
in all of those fourteen thousand little fields
each with its waterbed and drift of flowers.
It was quiet there. I heard silence swarming.
And liquid arrows bubbled inside my eyes :
yellow and molten, red and violet and blue.
Soon I will have to go, walking fast to reach
the five o'clock ferry back to Ros an Mhíl.
And then the bus to Galway and that banal,
savage bird, Shannon to Stansted. Not that
I wanted to, Máirtín : I'd rather stay here.
I eased my body under an upturned coracle
its blue-tarred carcass, then the sky above.
Now it's time to leave your house, I'll blow
you one more kiss, although you might not
want my kiss : this is what I came here for,
these words, the stone sleepers, language
that matters, language that can say 'yes'.
And the swell of real time against shores
of inhabited space.

But Now I Live On A Sorrowful Planet

But now I live on a sorrowful planet
Frida Kahlo

I should have worked as a porter in a remote hotel
or at the night-desk of a dour metropolitan hospital
I should have driven lorries before dawn down the
                    arteries of a weeping city
I should have handled tube trains into stations like
                    squealing pigs
I should have worked in a laundry or navvied it as
          the foreman of a brickies' troupe,
I should have been a laughter-clown or trapezed my
          life up your wide sistering streets.
Ah, but for now I just live on a sorrowful planet!
I should have got up before dawn and gone to the
          mosque, to the women's entrance,
                    being a woman,
I should have portered in hospitals or given singing
          lessons in oncology,
I should have run backwards up moorland meadows
          and gone raving over the blackberry
                    hill,
I should have closed my eyes in the face of oncoming
          tides, in the face of the patinas of
                    'no',
I should have tautened my nerves on the rage of
          exhausted ligaments,
I should have belly-danced under g-nomes or taken
          the cholesterol count of stem cells.

I should have looked at myself in the eyes of a monkey,
in the eyes of a dog,
I should have tied yellow ribbons on walnut branches,
I should have let myself collapse in the apricot valleys
of the highest sierras –
Ah, but I did none of these things, I painted the sun
as source of all energies, the rampant goddess
as swirl of life, the dog of my dreams,
the snake of all breath ...

Birds Of East London

When you live on the twenty-first floor of a tower
and way past midnight you hear a fracture
of wings and in the morning there's
a collar-dove on your balcony

is that a dream ?

When you live on the twenty-first floor and you get
home just at dawn from a party – or you've
been working at the desk all night, the
desk of words I mean – and the
mist you've travelled
home through

lies

flannelled just beneath
your feet so you cannot see the
ground and yet the whole
sky is king-fissure
blue

from the palest horizon to the most golden baroque

is that also a dream
but is it not also
the most real ... ?

And out of such skies come birds and bombs ...

When you live on the twenty-first floor and you
notice that in a crack in the cladding
a few metres down a kestrel
has made her nest

and when you see that kestrel
pinioned on its wing-bone, sitting at ease in
the middle air, shifting sideways on sudden
gusts – its unperplexed ligaments
ready to dive it through
skies of reality

through torn webs of nerves

and when you catch
the feather of the collar dove
floating past your eye ...

is that not a dream and
is life only a dream ?

Or when you see Arctic geese flying beneath your feet
toward the landing stage on the Camargue just
as once you saw them flying

between the mountain and the sea – in
the gap between sight and nothing
right there above your head –
on those far islands of
mica schist

way out west and beyond
the times of
clearance

is that only a dream or does life
just dream us ?

And language has broken down, language has been
bandaged – like the sun, like the bandaged
sun – and we speak in chunks
of betrayal words

when language itself
has become ...

Or when at eye level from your balcony you see black
darting swifts mewing in the fine drizzle or
turning their sleek bodies in the
sun as they bite tiny insects
simply for sustenance

is this just a dream of
life ?

Or the gannet that plunges down cliffs of light
(as a broke lift might through shafts of
darkness) and breaks the surface
of the curdled water leaving
its tongue's graffiti on
the shoal beneath

having picked out just one fish
for its gizzard and gullet

O my toppled sanity : O my maytime
market : O my bridge of
dreams

Or as a cormorant might
fly straight into the sun
and either it will crinkle and fizz in the black
heats – or else it will heal the sun's
bandaged
wound :

(for this is what birds know that we
no longer know)

Or the stormy petrel sleeping on the heave of
the ocean, giving countenance to
the wreck and the wrack
waiting for the spigot or flag
of seaweed or the onrush of
maritime tide

One time in my house on the burnt island a wren
deep-dived by a buzzard fled in through
my blue open door but then was as
bone burst by human space
as by any beak or claw

though I spoke to it
in bird words from the piece of
my hearth

and I cupped it in my hands
until off it flew

but my mind is a burnt island : as is
everyone's in this bruised
world, or in this world
of bruised minds

and is everyone just a
dream ?

When you live on the twenty-first floor and the old
Ukrainian man twelve floors down keeps
racing pigeons on his balcony –
Popa he is called
and he sings
lullabies
in

the sunlit pub on Cable Street
the pub that is not yet
shut down –

and

his pigeons fly in wide arcs, in circles
from his balcony, but they cannot
return him to the village
near Lv'ov (shhh
shhh :

this is his mother hugging him close
shielding his eyes, clasping him
to her body lest he moan
or whimper when
the partisans
piss in

the bushes she's hiding him in as
they pass through the
burnt village :

shhh ... shhh)

Is this then just a dream ?

Or when you live on the twenty-first floor and
you see two cormorants sweeping the sky
making wide arcs of their own choice
bargaining with no-one and
compromising nothing :

what in their bone structure
do they know that we will never
know ?

what in the balance between
their gut and their eye ?

and suddenly from sweeping the city they
streak and scud from one
sector of the city to
another

from one skerry to the
burning sun

(corporations named cars after animals, governments
named bombs after birds)

even language has its final answer, even
words fail – or else soar –
where we most need them

even birds fly in East London
coming from Iceland or the Western Isles
going to Morocco or Algeria or
south of the Sahara ...

Is this just a dream ?
this
parliament of birds, these
migrations

this flight path of swifts and swallows
this discourse on the sanities
this journey to be made
across breath

or

the stupidity of ever drawing
boundaries

When you live on the twenty-first floor and down
there in the paved market you can see
your friends ...

For My Friend, Max Sebald

Tell them I had a wonderful life
Ludwig Wittgenstein

Two months ago I was
talking to you in the Lithuanian forests : telling you
how old women from out of Druskininkai were walking
the blue floors of those stretched oceans with buckets
of mushrooms and moss

There space is old, trees are tall, memory is pain,
history is full of partisans and a sufi music conjures all
of us to whirl where the stalks of the forest barely sway.
I sensed you there because of the rotting of the music
and I knew you'd care.

Your room still is full of photographs
your realm looked after by trees. You who eschewed all
computer trails have been taken away by a skidding wheel
by black ice or a seizure of the heart, lifelong discourse
and your daughter's hurt

All I can do now is stagger
round my rooms mewling out your name Max, Max :
what will happen to language now, now you are not here
and who is left and how many remain of the anarchists
on the ice-floes of speech

These last weeks I had been
writing you postcards in my head : Max come to Whitechapel.
Come soon. Come and talk. Come and walk. Where are you ?
Why did you ? : but this has become an explosion of words
on the scarp of my pain

We'd talked about walking
from my village to yours : cutting a section across the Alps
or a section through a glacier's brain. From Precasaglio
in the Alta Valcamonica to Wertach in the Allgäu.
              Now I will do that without you.

        Before we met and surely ever since
we've been talking to each other. And even when the other
was not there we'd carry on in monologues to hear. I shall
go on talking to you for as long as my mouth can speak :
            or what is the point of language

           From where did I come
to this scarred field : you first heard my voice in your car,
you last lost your own voice there : what silence in the water,
what bird-smoke, what rough circle in our language has
            brought us back to here ?

        Dear friend, what is the use of speech :
I now asking of you questions you can no longer reach –
yet as you drift off to the snow-hole of your hills I hear
you say "they are ever returning to us, the dead" –
           Max, I am listening ...

Old Women Of My Childhoods

Every time I walk
Into an alley plunged in black sunlight
I remember old women from my childhoods

Their long dresses
Their crêpe skin that amazed me
The tiny flowers in the bowl of their faces
The black shawls when they worked
Their meadows, their fields and gardens
Silence that contained only answers of
Those old women plunged in sunlight

And from my first childhood
And circle of sunlight in the flower garden
And the daisies grown higher than my head
And my mouth that went through the fence
To kiss the mouth of the curly girl next door
And the magnified grasses when I lay
My face on the earth's soil

   And in my next childhood
And the one that came after my first
And was consumed with isolation and with
         the insane pursuit of premature
                     sanity

The one I spent schooled in order
   that torn childhood when line and colour
   were forcibly parted from language

In this new and easily come-by childhood
Every time I walked through an alleyway
held tight in the drizzles of soft rain

Every time this happened I
remembered the old women of
                    my childhoods

My aunt from
the city of china and canals
pottering in her goods yard
craving snowdrops from coal
kettles from coal-dust

Look!
She's bringing out the tin
bath to sud out all her bulges :

She who played
cricket with me in the garden
and read me bed-time stories

My grandmother in her long dress
Standing in the sun of another country
Standing in the militancy of her mildness

Standing like an alley plunged in light
A route to the future and not the past
In her lucid disregard for good sense

And my mother who
By the time of my third childhood
Had entered the last years of her own
And already herself was old

My mother then
I thought of almost as a child
Shopping for fresh pasta and winter coats
With her father in the shops of Frith
                    Street

And in those years
I carried her once in my arms
Up steep meadows to the mountain hut
And cooked for her as she for years
Had done the same but more
                    for me

And in my third childhood
the one that comes before the fourth
the one that is predicated on all the sanities
                    of madness
on all that is disreputable and indissoluble
& protests and proteins timed on youth

And in my final childhood
And that of the insanity I have yet to attain
Whenever I hobble into alleys of sunlight
And whenever I walk through walls
Through their non-existent holes
Into the drivel of words and
                    the palaver of farewells

I remember the old women
Of my childhoods and my early years
And of all the years I have put together
Shattered in alleys & plunged in black light

And when I dribble my goodbyes
And when I forget the arts of parting
I think back on my grandmother
Held between nutmeg and mountain birds
Held between polenta and a fistful of cloves
Held just where history exploded her

And in the later years
Those when the afterbirths of childhood
Had been thrown aside and not wrapped round
To heal memory or poultice political wound ...

And when the line of white on
My unshaven face is like a brittle field
Of hoar-frost with pecking birds

In those later years
I want to think back on the lives of
old women I have known ...

My grandmother
standing amazed and certain in her
superb seventeen years beauty

My grandmother standing
out of sepia with her eldest children
dressed in white for the camera
my mother also standing and
looking out through thick thin
turbulents of brown time

My grandmother
Leaning on her leaning stick

On the arm of my aunt
The amazed compassion of her youth
Still smiling from out her face ...

Is that what is meant by migration ?

A smile moving from one face to another ...

My grandmother
Was an economic migrant in time of war
Losing two babies at the border post
To the fiction of disease and
Unnecessary papers

Is that what is meant by asylum ?

I also with my words plunder matter :

Am I then master of what matters ?

Or old women
I knew in the Western Isles
Who never in their lives left their island
Nor even one township of it nor
Hardly even a hearth

But for summer pasture on the shieling moors ...

Or to handle herring on other eastern shores
Fingers cold-charred with gluey fish-scales ...

And yet the candour of their mouths
And yet the clamour of their justice ...

Or in my next childhood
And in my last but one when I had learnt
To count by a different system through this life
Through this stubborn uninhibiting uninhabitable
                    festering of breaking things

When even breath had become a betrayal
And language was a midden-heap of maggots
                    and worms

Or in the final childhood I will never attain
When we come to realise all the beautiful insanities
                    of compassion

And I managed fully to lose my sanity
Only whilst fully managing to retain it

And in this way I was able to walk again
Into the dark alleys of black sunlight

And to remember the old women of my childhoods

And therefore to crease out the lines of my life

And the palpable imbecility of ever drawing
                    boundaries

Brick Lane Mela Poem

Ghosts come pouring out the houses
                words have clogged
my throat : this mild winter I'll put
on my mountain scarf and go out in
                the dark :

I'll slowly walk down the slight curve
                and incline of the Lane,
my hand in the hands of my friends in
a tight drizzle towards the fizz of far
                light

Toward the tunnel of dark air that
                is neither light nor real,
but either must be Bethnal Green or
else is Beani Bazaar or the relic of a
                curling dream

And as I walk I am talking to ghosts
                and they are
my friends and they answer with mild
herbs of speech to calm me, as surely
                as I shamble

Past the oast-houses and mud fields of
Shuttle Street
and even as I curve back on Woodseer
a tinsmith is hammering cups next
to Banglatown C&C

And a man is pushing a trolley through
Sylhet Town
and I'm become as old and young as I am
and I float in curved space in the black
light of this lane

Here is Kafka's Dora who opened a café
with her brother
at 53 Brick Lane after the war. Here's
the string shop intact with its window
nailed to the moon

And my friend Nazrul Islam, the one
who wrote 'Vidrohi'
on the back of his hand. I am talking
to ghosts as I talk to my friends and
here in her car

Comes Shamim Azad, just in time as I
treat myself to a bowl of dhall :
join me dear friend, help coax lemon in
the lentil or fold the curd and unbone
the ilish-fish

And here is Nazrul Naz buying papers
           at the last Sangeeta
translating Obaidullah while the whole
vortex of Brick Lane rears up and curls
           round on its circle

Bill Fishman walks due south talking
           to his dead dad,
Majer Bogdanski plays his violin stood
in the middle of the Lane and no-one
           wants to complain

I walk out in the dark light of the road
           & hear the rotting of a sufi music
and I fall apart – or how else would I find
the mad-rapt sound I need and nowhere
           else can find

Let me hear music or I will not go mad
           and I want to lose
this sense and arthritis and spinning tin
of rationed time that ends and begins
           just where the Lane

Disappears : let me loose all sense or I'll
           not see what's looming
at the edge or hear the singers in the Mela
or taste the clay-baked fish and lassis of
           this swimming street

Raw musics burst in my head and make
stilt paths for my feet
as I shamble histories on this rooted coil
and seek the ever-precious venoms of
the curly snake

David Rodinsky walks by hand in hand
with Rachel
Lichtenstein : and Miriam Nelken rides
her drunken bike on toward the flower
meadows of her mind

Jeff Perks painted Brick Lane seamless
as a garment,
Avrom Stencl's sat beneath a thorn tree
talking to the birds and the drunk men
pelted with night's rind

Look at how they shine in the resident
air, yet no-one
sees them – because they are not there :
but I know they are & think of them
ghostly, ghostly

I see Dan Jones & Polly & Pola Uddin
outside Café Naz :
It was the cinema where anti-Nazis met.
Look : Tassaduq Ahmed has stopped
in the road to talk.

North of all time and of sound a lion cub
        is nose-sniffed
by a hair-singed hound : and just around
the edge a singer staggers in amongst
        hob-nailed boots

In the Knave Of Hearts market women
        and men drink away
the cold, while outside street kids talk to
donkeys and invisible singing birds
        perch on nothing's

Branch and in the Bar, men and women
        lift glasses that are half-full
and Markéta Luskacová frames their lives
with pilgrims and holy wanderers from
        the nomad world

Or by sleet-fires the aged young take
        their tinnies and their tea,
burning cardboard on palettes of wood
because nobody else knows what it's
        like to have stood

In the exact phases of their lives. Peace
        to their blood, as
to their eyes : they are ghosts of whom
I speak, song-birds sit in their duffelled
        hoods

And the Chicken Man of Leyden Street
car-washes
bloodied feathers from off his dungarees,
then ups and buys warmed beigels that
ooze cream-cheese

Up Sclater Street men as old as me gob
on bacon butties
and from enamel cups off table tops –
like all of us have always done – drink
pints of tea

Back in the mela-storm of the day I'll
nip into the Meraj or
my Sweet & Spicy and write this poem
on dough-fresh chapatti in milli-script
until it's done

And up above, the round filled moon is
clay-baked bread,
as if Kolkota Sukanto had not died young
or beautiful Jibanananda was living still
in Barisal

Then he'll take this world and place it in
its turning clay or
microwave it til the darkening of the day
until it glints and pecks like songbirds
in wet trees

Or when the city gets up off its knees
                    to weep
and tower blocks shed their pastel skins
and walk beyond the herded city limits
                    in sheets of sleet

I'll think back to this clay & sand and
                    brick-limned lane
back through ha'penny candle-lighters
and silk attics and weaver birds and
                    straw floors

And mulberry fruit and horse manure
                    and way-paths
winding through suburb fields, and mud
and more and the housing of the mad
                    & all of human betrayal

And wattle & pleasance & jugular woad
                    until I pull myself from
such streams to strudel from the all-night
baker's or burfi and jelabi from Ambala
                    & Alauddin

This street's become the river of our spate
                    and all of us are flowing :
all the living and the dead who congregate
eeling a way through life & maelstromed
                    outside doubt

As we walk along the middle of the lane,
                    all cars banished,
all traffic body, blood and unboned cloth
gone in the trick of music, or the magic
                    of the mela

Such fish we are here : slabbed carp with
                    blinded eyes, raw dog-fish,
stilt-walking fish and neon-ray-fish, deep-
mud fish and perch and pike, and then
                    a dream of hilsa

And here somewhere between midnight
                    and the dawn – in
the heat of it and nearly at its heart, all of
pain and succour and the bone mounted
                    beneath our skin

All the cream of it, all the ice-cold of it,
                    here where we stand and
raw history gushing us past on the river
of our street, not holding back coiling
                    waters of our spate

Praha Poem

* 1

The high walls of Vojanovy Sady
Opposite the house of the poet Holan

Behind one the medieval cantata
And the may-time conference of the birds

And behind the other :
Centuries of silence, broken wings and
The dark pain of the moon child

What more can be said, little one :

Almost mathematically
That as much as once we loved

We now hate

* 2

As soon as I got to Prague
I went to Anagram just off Týn

And bought Tomaž Šalamun's
Ballad For Metka Krasovec

I knew it would be there :
Metka and Tomaž are married
(or were when last I heard)

Then I got drunk on the Jakubská
And the fogs of Praha came over me

All week I slept entirely alone. Even
That may be a slight exaggeration.

* 3

Stephen, you are losing yourself

The two cafés you best remember
Rough ones with scratches and benches
(one close by the Kampa, the other off
Konviktská, and both up alleys) are
Shut and being done up for trade.

You've bought two books :
A small edition of Nezval's *Básně noci*
And something of Giacometti's prose
Just because you wanted to : no
      better reason.

Stephen, you are losing yourself.
The woman who loved you has left you.
Surely you must know that. Go out
Into the wheat fields of Europe
      And sleep.

* 4

Frightening this hatred
This passionate un-love for
Someone you still love

Who was the abuser, who the abused ?

Or is it true that both of you still ...

Love each other I mean and therefore
Hate the logic of living that has so

Bludgeoned love to death

* 5

No. Truth is
That in this city I have destroyed
Whatever I once knew of a woman
Whose existence I had deranged
And whose existence had
Deranged me.

* 6

The night of
The Ceremonial Banquet
At the Monasterial Brewery (Strahov Courtyard 302)
I went home early to Mrs. Vorlíčková's
And had cold starters and Budweiser in Na Tetíně

Just before its kitchen closed

Strange isn't it, little one
Those we love the most
Are the ones we end up hating, precisely because
They are the ones we most love

We who aborted each other
In the absolute impatience of our angers
In the intricate tearing of our nerves

* 7

I have come to
Praha (Nusle District, tram no. 11)
Seemingly to break down or else to avoid so doing

I have run screaming from the conference
And the best moments have been drinking wine
On the Míšenka just round the edge
From the house of Vladimír Holan

I can't speak any more.
I have long abandoned the science of conversations.
I crave just one day in the Moravian spring.
I look forward to the town of Olomouc, to friends
And sleeping and talking about Ivan Blatný.

* 8

The year I disappeared into the Moravian country
Was the best year of my whole and my unwhole life

Those who joined me spoke only of the High Tatra
Those who took me apart managed somehow to put me
                                together again

* 9

In all the time
I was in Praha
I never once walked out to the suburbs
Or took a tram to its end-stop

Little one,
What is it about anger
That drives pain in on its tendered self
Coiling and then slamming prejudice
            into the coma of love ?

* 10

No, that is not true.
Each day I jumped the tram to its terminus
To the bistro at Ďáblice, the bus-shelters of Spořilov
Or the proletarian estates of Hurka

What is it about anger
That drives knowledge away from the brain

What is it about blood
That drives it pulsing to the cunt
Beyond the archive of the eyes

Little one

* II

In the afternoon heats
I fled both myself and the mid-city traumas
And went up to the eating-house above Troja

Wave on wave of anger pulsed through me

All of the hatreds piling up
Were balanced back by the dark
Garden yard of the immigrant bistro,
The owner who spoke Turkish, Arabic,
Czech, Kurdish, English, Persian
                    at the very least

And the site workers taking time off
To watch Republika Czecha getting through
Their semi-final, smashing Sweden at ice-hockey
In the quietest of all noisiest rooms

* 12

The blue beads
Round your neck, little one
Are what cannot translate time

They are the tiny fish-hooks
That lodged themselves inside me.
In the sea-swirl of the labia and clitoris
They are also flesh of me

* 13

These Moravian hills and trees
These horizons of white writing
These church villages and rape fields

This rush of green to the west and the water
This loss of both silence and anger in the harshest
Of all language, in the angers of love ...

* 14

You millions of trees in the Pardubice meadows
You branches of lilac in the Moravian spring
You bent down women digging early potatoes
You teenage girls fishing carp in mild May ponds
You streams and scarp slopes and spruce stands
You firs and eagle hawks flirting brown wings

* 15

What a superb rainstorm
Over the mushroom fields of Bohemia

What an atrocious downpour
Across the lonely rail-yards of Europe

All the roads become rivers
The rivers become roads

Come little ones, children,
Kurds and you without country or wall

Come and drink from these wet ruts
These generous fountains for the speechless

Or Heaven has come too soon
In these meadows not so far from Terezin

* 16

City on the hill
Train rushing west into the bloodshot night
Sky that must be menstruating
Unrequited curve of the delineated earth
River that is a perfect reflection of its skies

When I stroke you
Blood that pulses beyond the archive of your eyes
When I stroke you what coils and then falls back
Is the violence of our breathing

Reach out, little one, touch me

* 17

Those last days in Praha
I found some money in a hole in the wall
That was a bitter better stroke of luck

So I went to play pool in the Café Louvre
And then looked for the poetry of silence in
The alleys behind Husova and Na Perštýně

Later I went out to Palmovka on the tram
And stayed drinking in the tenement blocks
Out there & in Na Kotlářce and Na Hájku

Until the dawn tram chairlifted me to Žižkov
And the blood sun rose upon another day

* 18

O you matted frescoes of St. Kliment
I was sucked out of this city in thin tubes
I was womb-hoovered of my love

What was left in the airport bin-bags
Was the throbbing artery of time

Little one

My Grandfather Worked In Pizza Express ...

My grandfather worked in Pizza Express in Greek
Street in 1904

Except it wasn't Pizza Express then, it was Crameri
& Caruso's Italian Coffee Parlour

And my grandfather was second-head waiter and my

Mother was not far off being born in Phoenix Street in
the tenements opposite the theatre, the tenements
that were there until the seventies, until that is

They were pulled down & something else was put up
in their place, because it was regeneration time

And there's a photograph of her peeping round from
behind the ice-cream vendor's barrow as
if she knew what was to come

And every Sunday she'd go with her mother & father
to the red church in Soho Square

The church where a piece of cornice fell off & clipped
the biretta of a passing priest, o that priest
will pass by there no more,

And every Thursday for years after they'd moved to
the Creamery out in West Croydon – the one
in the arcade opposite the station

Every Thursday my grandfather'd take his daughter,
my mother, back into Soho to get the gossip,
the fresh pasta & spinach

And they'd sit in Lui Crameri's, he talking dialect with
his cronies, she squashed stiff into a windowless
corner unable to squeak

That same year Stalin & Lenin were over-nighting it
in Tower House in Fieldgate Street over here
for the 3rd International

And the Italian anarchists of Dean St. & Clerkenwell
glistened as they waited under the dewy moon
with greased daggers drawn

Hoping with surety that what would happen could be
swayed and vectored out of sync so that their
century might not have been

What, of course, it had to be. But no : it couldn't, it
couldn't, it simply couldn't be !

My grandfather painted ceilings somewhere in Soho,
bright with mountains in the sunlit snow &
virgin spirits in their peacock shrines !

And I stand here now in Fieldgate Street watching as
a corner of zinc flies from the coppice roof to
land by my unflummoxed feet

And I take the found zinc object as a door-stop for my
hearthless home – we who have to live in some
new degenerate regeneration zone

And as I eat my *fiorentina* in Frith Street I remember
all of this, and all I can say to the waitress who's
asking 'Would I like another coffee yet'

Is 'what is the number of this century we are living in'
& 'how did we get to where duplicity is become
the ordinary nature of our breath ?'

& 'political hurt can hurt us no more' & 'the noise of
the heart is a furtive claw' & 'the remote places
are the heart of our world'

& 'the colours of blood are war-flags unfurled' & 'the
war against terror is an error of fear' & 'all
of us shimmie toward ordinary death'

Then I paid & rushed out penniless into the peacock-
shrieking street, flummoxed to know I'd
met exactly who I'd had to meet.

Cheshire Street

Among all the rakers of Cheshire Street, among the
                 traders in bananas & apples
off tressel-tables on street corners, among dealers in
Doc Martens and plimsolls under mild autumn suns,
among villains & wreckers & backyarded emperors,
          where the neurotic bookseller used
to deal in toxins and leather, where you could barter
old negatives for a coin or a kiss, where you might be
able to find postcards of your grandmother or pastels
                 of some orange grove,
or photographs of banditeering Kurds from Saqqez,
under the mild sun where you could remember snow,
under a mild sun where you could not predict 'now',
                 under the mild sun in
your own unpredictable mildness, attacking no-one!
In Blackman's bootshop, in Majer's street of dreams,
                 in the kingdom of Charlie Burns,
in the market where John Sheehy came after leading
his donkey over from Ealing on the epic journey that
          lasted four & forty years & many pubs:
                 I ask you! I am telling you!
                        Now! ...
Among the rare rakers & pullers of Cheshire Street.
          Along with Alan Dein in
the mild October sun, along with Rachel Lichtenstein.
In the traumas of memory & the little nauseas of time
where old bombs fell and new bombs will be hatched.
In those most mild of airs, those most soporific suns!
          Suddenly I plunge south into
the river of dreams and lean into the cave of memory,
and contort myself through unmanageable portals,

through the space that isn't there,
but is ! And then after
decades suffered in the reflexes of tar, I rise gasping
through the bubbles of the deep stream : and look ! –
Cheshire Street is gone,
the bridge of dreams is gone, Majer & the market are
gone, the mountains of blood are gone, the donkeys of
memory are gone, the body in the glacier is gone,
our bodies that go
are gone !
And rising through bubbles of deep time I can see :
blank faces with blunt eyes in shaman-trance,
skin-peeling back the dancer
from the dance

Early Morning Visit From David Silver

David Silver came round again today
Early, after a gap of five or six years

His Irish woman from Coventry's gone
He's back on the fags but off the booze

And saved a thousand pounds & more
& lost nine hundred papering his door

He's still at 50 Dominie Road, Bow E3
Two televisions (one big, one small), a

Table, settee-set, fridge, no washing
Machine, cooker (but he never cooks),

Meals-On-Wheels on seven day-tickets,
A giro weekly & monthly though quite

Why he's never really known. A Social
Worker calls in on Tuesday every week

She's Finnish & good, with trousers, he
Says : like a beatnik with a leather coat.

Kind heart and head, and hands to help
Fill out his forms & tell him to stay still.

David's got a kitchen, bedroom, a hall,
Bathroom and as he says a living room

A double-bed though he's always alone,
A sink, a tap, a radio-video, a telephone,

One joey-budgie, no longer cat or dog :
The ginger latter run over, some catter

Got the cat, or else it just went its way.
Who in this life anyway is here to stay ?

His goldfish jumped out from its bowl
And fell between a dustpan and a stool

His mum & dad are long gone & dead
One brother married, he's pretty sure :

He went to the wedding. Not seen any
Brother or sister in about twenty year.

One of them's a ginger beard, glasses.
The other lost his wages on the horses.

He asks me for a letter with its stamp
Part so he can copy down my address

Part because he likes the yellow shape
And part so he can get a friend or his

Finnish social worker to write out what
He wants to say to me : David himself

Can neither read nor write : a dunce
He says but I say no dunce just badly

Taught, never put back from truancy
Or ever schooled for unskilled living.

What is a truant in this ordered life, if
Not a beggar-man or poor giving-thief?

He asks me is he fifty-nine or sixty yet:
Born March 20th 1944: I say fifty-nine

But add he is whatever he wants to be,
He's free to choose, to be or not to, but

In the glut of a queue, of course he's not.
Freedom's just a token given to the few.

He says his neighbours are all cheats &
Robbers, some chickling aimed a rocket

Through his door-flap last Guy Fawkes
Night that burnt down bed and bedroom

And put him out of house but now he's
Back and in the daily rhythm of his lack

He wants to take my bust alarm-clock
With large numbers printed on its face

He wants me to be his pen-friend since
He hardly ever comes to Shadwell now

He gives me fifty p because he couldn't
Give me any for my birthday or a card

And says his Social Worker's told him
About classes in music, cars & cooking

At One-Stop Shops and old Town Halls
Or learning how to read & how to write.

He's lit up a fag and I've said that's fine
Though I don't like smokes in my home

And I've not wanted this poem to rhyme
Though it could but what'd be the point

It's not as if our lives have such order :
I've a fiver in my pocket (plus fifty p !)

And no knowing when the next is due :
I don't care whether I eat or sleep at all

Or if anyone reads this poem any more.
I write it as it makes me happy in time

Of war. Anyone with any sense can hear
An inner rhythm ticking against my fear.

Next month I'm going to Galway to read.
Maybe that's where David's lady's gone

But I'll not see her there I'm pretty sure.
David himself likes pure history books &

Takes the picture ones from his library :
A lending van on wheels but its blue door

Opens him shut with knowledge and puts
A dunce's cap on every time it takes it off

He's stopped drinking now but buys all
His food and juice from an Offie close-by

His home in Bow. Bow : Bow of the Bells
Bow of the Match Girls, Bow of the Cows

That once got milked up tin churn alleys.
Bow of the Quadrants, Bow of the Attics,

Rich Bow, Poor Bow, Beggar Bow, Thief.
Bow ... Bo ... Bah ... Beh ... Blah ... Baah.

When he leaves my home (he had been up
The London for a blood-test that was why

He'd come this way) having found me here,
Turns to wave as I stand at my open door

And I'll wait for the first card/letter from
The first pen-friend I've had since I was 8

'Sorry I can't always come round to visit,
I will try to send you a birthday card next

Week : I get a month's money about then.
I'm going to get myself a washing machine

Or try to. I could send you a clothes parcel
If you are short of trousers. A friend at 48

Is writing this for me. I've got to go & buy
A stamp album to start saving stamps. I'll

Send this from 50 Dominie Road, E3 4EN
& bless you, David S., your true old friend.'

And then he adds but doesn't know if I will
Get off at Mile End then find the Cemetery.

Ask for Dominie Road & just cut through.
Come with a stick but be not blind. I'll try.

I've chimed this poem on the years he's had
I'm not bothered with rhyme but – so what

I've written this just for what David's got ...

Meditation At The Window

The anarchist alleys where Avrom Stencl walked
bright in sunlight dark with sun's battered work
new cobble-stones full with language yet & words.
Alleys where the false historians lurk, their hardhats
gurgling festivities of sullen centenary grief.
Or the real alleys where Bill Fishman stops to talk.

I think of the friends who've known this angry world :
then see them all walking here fast beneath my eyes.
See them seething : Ivan & Alan, Rachel & Daniele.
Know this planet is a little sphere, this tiny pin-prick
where we look & see our blood-flows pattern stars.
Look ! There's old Ahmed pulling his trolley home.

And as I stand here meditating at the open window
looking over at bare walls and abandoned vaults &
workshops where a year ago my friend hammered tin
I'm also standing wherever else I've been, at windows
looking over stunned and inland seas, at windows
opening onto mountain valleys and cherry orchards
at windows overlooking the churn of urban screams.

And when I stand here meditating with Theo in my
arms, this fifteen months old guy who looks at me &
charms the bird-words out of my branching mouth :
We look and see blue sky or stars or rucksacked men
or corporation carts, gangs of girls or coloured cars,
but say to each other 'look there's fox going home'.
Then we walk, me holding him, he holding me and
making new geometries we venture out to see how
the star-sparkled world is doing in its absence.

We talk and hang on tight in this world where words
prevail and silence is looked askance and meditation's
thought to be some poor alternative to an assault rifle.
We all walk alone, thin as breath or hair, flake or bone
we all walk to the seething stations or finish beneath
mountains that hold snows through heat-raw summer.
But I want to say poetry is a vital art, pumping bright
blood through our heart, poetry is laughter, poetry is
breath. Poetry's a translation out of silence and, for
sure, translation's the opposite of making war.

My Mother, Her Tongue

When the body leaves the body with such
        suddenness, such speed,
when there is no time to draw a face, to say
a word, to hold a voice in memory – where
        are you gone ?

I went into your garden and walked on its
        brittle grass : the little
trees were stiff with frost and the sun drank
milk from the pewter of its glass, o mother
        white as jasmine

I cupped the shaman's cup in my hand &
        tossed it to and fro,
your body has become these rancid flowers
that in the night-time glow, but where now
        are you ?

Birds came to me in that garden – swallows
        turning their high bellies –
they spoke to my fingers with their tongues,
they filled the air, inside my head and out,
        but where are you ?

Car of death that moves off at the speed of
        the living,
car of death that moves off at walking pace,
unendured pain of peace, sun wrapped
        in its own linen

Wisteria and summer honeysuckle melted
                their scents in that yard,
jasmine and lilac, basil and mint and apple,
grasses that were magnified beneath my
                eye where I lay ...

Horses drifted into that garden way past
                midnight : they nuzzled
the windows and the door. I saw their hoof
prints in the snow : what dream was that,
                mother of jasmine

As a child I was happy in the garden of your
                house : through
an air of daisies taller than my head to where
a tiny sun shone through the milky belly
                of a horse

There was a litany, a bright effacement,
                you were there who
were no longer there, seamstress-swallow
pulling needles of air through the cloth
                of my sight

Little fish of the midday sun, little fish in
                the air swimming,
little fish that gobbled oxygen and insects,
I see you turn high up over your wing
                to look down at me

I see you fling the blue vocable 'never' with
                its dull meaning against
the void of the sky where it explodes colour
in the space where nothing happens, o you
                in the summer of jasmine

When your ashes were scattered you became
those flowers, you became
these trees, you became those birds that fling
their songs across torn webs of sky leaping
from goblets of light

You are not ashes, you are a tree unfurled
from where the soil and air
are slung against a silent wind that folds me
back from despair, o language coming from
you white as jasmine

You've flown between the frost and the sun,
you never were ash
in the charnel-house, the ordinary guards of
death had no meaning before the jasmine
of your face

Now your body is gone and your discourse,
your spirit like a bird is flown,
I strain to measure your voice in my lungs
but I know colliding rivers have loosed
my mother tongue

I was not there when the bird of your soul
flew off from your body, I
could not watch that final trance and when
I was late come your breath was no longer
making

Its slow unmeasured dance across the floor,
when I got to your death your
mouth was already set in its trancing curve,
your nose was held and bent against those
jasmines of your face

I do not know if it was the struggle with
       the oxygen mask (you
trying to push that sudden strangler off)
or if it was the struggle to stay alive that
       stopped your breath

This body, this light, these words, this work :
       where are you now ?
What dialect of the mother-tongue rose into
your mouth before being reeled back to this
       fading dream ?

You took that sense to where your ashes
       flock as dancing birds –
you singing across blueness to those snows
where shaman meditate the dying of
       their sisters

What shaman words can sing against my
       dullness now ?
What melted core of language has stunned
my mother-tongue ? That slow lark rising
       from stiff snow

In its cliff-face field in mild January winds
       it's become the bird you,
weaving breath from under streamy cirrus
and the earth that seemed to stagger under
       me as you flew

You were a spinning top in front of an
       open fire : I was
watching colour fly and we were talking
and what was dull was melted down to
       this still measure

Car of death that moved at the speed of
        the living, car of death
that moved at a walking pace, unendured
pain of peace, sun that was wrapped in
        its own linen

When I came back to the house I knew you
        were still there –
though much of the house was gone – and
I cried out through the world's war to you,
        O mother white as jasmine

The house is blind without you inside : but
        I am lifting it as
a lantern and swing it through its barriers
of pain and there is affirmation in this
        graft of light

The house is blind without your eyes, but
        you are still there,
wrapping pancakes in lemon, tired limbs
in warm sheets, folding pastry on apple,
        roasting meats

The house is blind without your eyes, but
        I will walk in your
door and rub my face stiff with frost and
bring roses inside that will flower in your
        tender house

And I will bring pasta and mushrooms and
        spinach and aniseed loaves,
this time I will bake bread and pour coffee
from a green jug to feed you, as once you
        fed me

I will bring milk and polenta and red wine,
and mackerel with thyme,
sour-sweet apples from the garden, broccoli,
mint and burnt sugar : not enough, for all
you gave

You who lived fifty years in the same house
what happened when
you passed over to the language of silence ?
What dialect of the mother-tongue faded
from your face ?

In your last years your skin became as crêpe
paper is
and who knows but it was you wrapped inside
thinking on your nieces and your nephews
and your sons

Your face has irrevocably changed : I will
wipe clear the white
walls of your house and you will rise in flight :
bird of jasmine, tree of frost, starling burst,
glint of schist

Swallows are dancing above the barn-half in
the slow trapeze of the sky,
stretched cirrus is carded in the weave of air :
how is it possible that memory can travel
back so far ?

Your own mother is calling back toward you
in the plum harvest,
along the vine terrace, into the cow-house,
across the snows of calm or in the valleys
of the mountain

You are still in the barn-half of that house
            jumping from the threshold
down to steamy hay with milk-drunk calves
then running through the thick wood doors
                out to jasmine air

Dun cows walk past the blunt end of a byre
            and I can hear you hear
their belling necks then see their bellies sway
past as they veer out onto the pasture slope
                into jasmine air

And the red mountain collapses and the red
            mountain is still there,
and the red mountain is a road and is a river
and rises through my blood as melted mess
                held there as love

Because the dead do not die when they die,
            because the dead
always die when they die, because the shaman
of death is a bird in this translation of breath
                into words

One time I carried you the last few metres to
            the mountain hut. Now
your body is leaving you as you sleep and you
can see your waiting mother calling to you
                from the slope

You remember your childhood dialects as
            you die, their curt
abbreviations clinging close to breath, then
air lifts you and you look back at us from
                jasmine night

And I write this in happy memory of you :
a song to be sung,
a flight of birds across a burning sky, bare
feet on wet grass, aniseed loaves looped on
poles to dry

And I write this poem to celebrate you :
words white as jasmine,
a sutra for when the body's left the soul,
a song to be sung for the life-line of the
mother-tongue

Houses & Fish : Kite-Poem

I remember their

names :

Nabil, Shelina, Billie Blue, Lindsey, Nasima, Lynton, Habib, Aktar, Sayera, Raju, Michael, Julekha, Tara, Sadiqua, Samantha, Cashael, Roxanne, Abdul,

Davina Daniel, Abdul,

Nicola, Samantha,

Abu Anas, Gemma, Bablu,

I remember how they drew

stars and painted houses

And I remember the words

they painted onto their dreams

ordinary words, dream words

house, birds, star,

sand, moon, tree, bed,
flower, window

tree, flower, sun, fish

starfish, oldfish, eggfish,
coloured fish,
fish with ears

seaweed-fish, flower-fish

lion, bird, snake & snake's
brother & snake's sister

& snake-fish

I remember how they wrote
the obdurate delights of colour :

blue, red, purple,

bloa, rad, porpol :

I remember that
there were children called
michaelnabil and children
called julekhadavinagemmaabu

and armedeniel

And I remember how stars were painted
with hearts into their dreams

and how houses were faces and
that fish were cars
that could never
crash

that fish were houses and houses
were fish and how

we all of us swam through
the city with its

sky of mango and crushed
brick

and how shoals of tiny-fish coursed
in our blood
and cascaded through our
kidneys

and how plankton
that were cousins, aunts and
enemies fed
in the sluices
of our bellies

And I remember how these
five-year-olds played in
the yards

and how I'd be out there
                with them or

        how I'd look out from
                the staff-room first floor
                window

        kneeling on the desks
to see the whirling of stars and
                fish

        and how then we'd painted
        a banner full of
                summer colours

and then I'd sailed it north from
        Wapping to Aldgate

in and out the traffic floes
        negotiating calm

against the logic of journal-truth
        and government

with bread and history in my
        sack, with wet-fish

        and rock-salt, with pome-
                granate clusters,

with yeast-bursts and blueberry
                & memory

I remember their second names :

Mohammad Ali, Hussain,
Barnes,
Begum

Woodman, Rahman, Miah,
de Farias, Morgan

Hussein, Uddin,
Chambers,

Khan, Corrall, Mason,
Karim, Rahman,

Brown, Rippingale,
Piggott, Mukith,

Choudhury, Hibbard, Uddin,
Steele, Gayle

All of us stars constellated on
the board of the sky :

and where are we now ...

and where are we now ...

and where, and
where and where

are we now ...

Night Security Guard, Fieldgate Street

"But what are you doing there ?" I said
                    to him,
        stood on the scaffolding of the old
            Doss House's first floor,
    the clock moving its tight fists round
                way past midnight.

And as answer he gave me the title of my
        poem, even as I said to him :

        "I have to write this poem
    about this building, its absolute history,
    though no-one has asked me to & no-one
            is paying me for it, & about
    the lives of all the people who have ever
                stopped in here"

And saying this, he acknowledged me with
            the gratis of his hand :

So, "therefore" I said "where do I begin ?"

With the moon-faced girl sat by the grating
            of the ground-floor stairway
                past midnight ?

I said nothing, nonetheless she did say 'hello'

With the cats that scurried right through all
            the wee hours of the night ...

But they had carried off all the maritime air
that feeds the art of memory

"Where's justice in any of this ?" I said &
he laughed, but he was laughing
with & not at me at all

And the tenement shook with a century of
fiction.

He stood there as if near a café in Kraków.

He stood there as if outside Vaga Bookstore
in Geminidas Ulica in Vilnius.

He stood there as if his life depended on it.

He stood there as if he were wading through
snow, or as if snow were scraping his
scratch cards for him

He stood there as if he were trying to wrap
a condom round a chimney

He stood there as if 'autistic' & 'artistic'
were the same word – which
of course they are

He stood there as if time had never started
in any of the wide streets of Whitechapel
or certainly had never finished

I no longer knew where I had come from
or to where I was going ...

But suddenly, walking home, I looked back
and saw the future laid out like a toy
& it gleamed inside my eye

Necessary Presence

Gareth Evans

For those of us fortunate to have heard him, Stephen Watts is a remark-able public reader of his own poems and those by poets he admires. It might seem counter-intuitive to say this when considering his work in the context of a print publication, but it is critical to understanding what, how and why he writes. His passionate delivery – the rhythmic roll of the speaking voice in lines both rigorously constructed and free-ranging at once – contrasts unforgettably with his sitting or stand-ing quite still. What is constant throughout is the undeniable liveness, the fact of the happening. This is no rote recital. Watts' writing brings us closer to the living, rather than separating us by paper from it. Experience is embodied in both the event and the book. Writing is speaking is reading is breathing – literally.

Life is its own evidence; the enduring necessity of the moment experienced – an encounter with the undeniably real in time and space (together becoming place) – determines the record. But the poem is a living thing – that is to say, a breathing thing – *first*, and remains so, from initial phrasing to print to repeated reading, in the hands of the greatest writers. You can hear the inhale and the out in the spaces between phrases. As a *Guardian* masterclass blog reports, '"There's nothing mysterious about your prose style," says the author Kevin Barry, "it's a direct projection of your personality."' True enough, but trans-lating that into written 'voice' is the thing. When it comes, write it on scraps, envelopes, the edges of newsprint, in notebooks and other people's books; work on and repeat it, work on and repeat it out loud and in mind on the too slow journey home when the pen has dried up, the pencil broken. Find it later on scraps, envelopes, the edges of news-print, in notebooks and other people's books; in drawers and on discs and on drives. Re-member it. Embody it again as once it was viscerally felt. Style in this incarnation is insight.

Just as his beloved Thames rises and falls / falls and rises; just as the Uist he knew is a constant negotiation between sea and very low-lying shore, so Watts' poetry is in ceaseless exchange with the sources of its line. He really does take it for a walk – daily – among the high Alps where his mother's family came from, across damp peat fields, in the shadows of the towers of chrome and glass that refuse the weather of things on their slippery facades; towers he wishes might never again emerge from the morning fogs that sometimes obscure them entirely. Their silence is that of wealth and its myriad exclusions. He, on the counter edge, is witness, his purpose... protection, to and of the clamour of the majority world. He is kin to the angelic eavesdroppers from Wim Wenders' *Wings of Desire*, tuning in and wishing to calm the distress on the 21st floor or the despair of the city's harsh yards; to frame it and name it a little, in the having noticed to save its sometimes thread-bare grace, its everyday bruised gold: to raise its stakes in the gamble of making. His presence cannot be defined or fixed by clockwork mechanics. The city often makes the sense that it does (when it does) because of his appearance in that instance – as performer or observer, angered or smiling, as fierce with the false as he is sensitive to the sorrow, delighted by the delightful.

His own writing is DNA-interwoven with his roles as educator, translator, nurturer of obscured and often oppressed talent, whether distant across dictatorial borders or swept aside on homeless pavements closer to his day. Were he still in Scotland, he might have become the Makar; no matter, that is what he is, closer to Margaret Tait and her Orcadian expansive modesty – of marking but never of ambition – her poet-film-drawing practice, than to the procedural publishing pundits. It's wayward *and* way-making. It leaves the main path. Does he – like

Nick Drake – have a 'skin too few', feeling it all too much? Should we not say instead that he has a sense too sharp, too attuned to the truths of our times. Triangulating the poem with the place and purpose of its making, he maps a common ground of encounter we are all encouraged to attend.

This remarkable volume matters so much because, live readings apart, until very recently it has not been easy to find Watts' relatively few and occasional ventures into sustained print. He has been more widely represented by his translation titles and his acts as anthologist than by his own authored collections. Early volumes were chapbooks and pamphlets from lovingly dedicated micro-presses, with understandably tiny print runs. One 'selected' was not allowed to run its course.

That is not to say, of course, that his own poetry went unnoticed. Those who knew of it *sincerely* knew of it, not least the late W.G. Sebald, whose final novel *Austerlitz* (2001) quotes from Watts' 'Fragment' and features images, narrative threads and characterisation that could not have happened without their meeting and subsequent friendship (this has been well documented elsewhere, not least in Iain Sinclair's *Austerlitz and After: Tracking Sebald*, published by Test Centre in 2014).

In the last ten years the situation has steadily improved. *Mountain Language* and *Journey Across Breath* appeared, carefully twinned, from Hearing Eye in 2012. Enitharmon Editions published the substantial *Ancient Sunlight*, with a rallying cover endorsement from Sinclair, in 2014. What marked a sea change was Test Centre's first publication of *Republic of Dogs/Republic of Birds* in 2016, along with the rapturous response to this 'recovered' text from the 1980s. Reprinted in 2020 and now under Prototype's care, it has also been revisioned on film in the luminous 16mm essay *The Republics*, a pitch-perfect collaboration with film-maker Huw Wahl, whose mother published Watts' first ever collection decades earlier. Loyalties, longstanding affiliations, to people and to place; the journey and the time of the journey: this is core, this is the project.

The ecological worldview inherent in Watts' poetry – non-hierarchical, committed to 'relation', dedicated to the flora, the fauna, the more-than-human, the wild and stray – is matched by his approach to being in the world as a writer and artist. There is a vulnerability to this but also a suppleness and a vitality that unites poet, publisher, designer and reader. For those of us who have known his writing, this first collected works marks both the culmination of a long-held desire to read *through* the work from its beginnings and an unignorable artefactual realisation of the status and necessity of this *oeuvre*.

As John Berger always advocated, one's work must be *of use*. Stephen's work has survived, it has endured and now it can thrive. It sings the human at the heart of the capital and in the face of capital. It reminds the edges that they too are central. Intensely local, it is utterly international. Porous and grounded, precise and open: like the wind in the trees at night, it is both material and mystery. All the voices are here (the lost, the forgotten, the passed: they no longer are these things). This constellation of leaves (in both senses) is a shelter and a ladder from earth to sky, from the body to what cannot be held.

Watts' poetry is an invitation, in the fullest sense. Etymology is key here: it speaks not only of solicitation but also incitement, challenge, entertainment; of pursuing *with vigour*.

So Stephen invites you. You were and always have been welcome. We shall meet in the halls and the squares; on the valley's flank and the mountain's top; by the river, on the shore. We shall meet in the streets. They have always been ours. Perhaps we thought they were lost to us. Perhaps they once were. With this collection the resistance begins afresh. With this collection we are taking them back.

Bibliographic Note & Acknowledgements

This book has its immediate origins in various conversations with Jess Chandler at Prototype and I thank her wholeheartedly for her suggestion to collect together a span of my poetries, a sort of journey across breath. Later, but essential to the work of pulling everything together, Rory Cook joined the conversation and editing, and I offer him many thanks for all his work & insight. It mattered that two editors much younger than myself liked my work so much. We began bringing together poems from various books and journals, but I was also prompted to search out unpublished manuscripts, of which there are quite a number.

In one sense the idea of this book as a 'Collected Poems' is a precisely accurate description of my hope to see all these poems published at one time or another & 'collected' in the end : but both because a significant amount of previously unpublished poetry is included, and also because 'Collected' seemed a slightly pompous term, we've subtitled it 'Poems 1975–2005'. My great thanks to Jess & Rory for enabling this book to be published.

The arrangement and flow of the poems is more or less, though not entirely, chronological. Perhaps it helps to give a brief outline of their publication (& non-publication !) history :

Some of these poems first appeared in the following volumes (& some in more than one) :

The Lava's Curl
(Walsden: Grimaldi Press, 1990 & Swaledale Festival, 2002)

Gramsci & Caruso
(Olomouc: Periplum, 2003, with Czech translation)

The Blue Bag
(London & New Delhi: Aark Arts, 2004; repr. 2005)

Mountain Language/Lingua di montagna
(London: Hearing Eye, 2008)

Journey Across Breath/Tragitto nel respiro
(London: Hearing Eye, 2011)

Gramsci & Caruso
(Monza: Mille Gru, 2014, with Italian translation)

Ancient Sunlight
(London: Enitharmon, 2014; repr. 2020)

Some other poems appeared in (some of) the following journals, while others may have been published in journals, but I have forgotten which & where : *Approach Poets, Poetry Review, Long Poem Magazine, Crossing The Line, A Company Of Poets, Poetry Wales, Magma, Scarf, Test Centre, Banipal, Prototype*, and others. My thanks to all their editors.

Many other poems, though, appear here for the first time. Not because I didn't like them, or considered them unfinished, or didn't want them published : more that it just didn't happen that they were published & then they got put aside, or mislaid. Among these poems are : most of the poems in the sections 'The Birds' & Other Poems, 80s Poems, Strands, Clusters ... & Four Essays, including a number of the longer poems : 'Visions', 'Discourse With The Physicists', 'Stepney Poem' & the poem 'Strands, Clusters ...'.

The trajectory of published and unpublished poems is both simple and complex : my first book *The Lava's Curl* was hand-set and published by Amanda Ravetz at Grimaldi Press : we had originally intended to include about twice the number of poems, and even contemplated a second book, but the labour of hand-setting & printing that lovely book curtailed its contents. Most of these un-included poems form part of the 80s Poems section in the present book.

The Blue Bag – which is included here in its entirety – was first published by Sudeep Sen at Aark Arts in 2004, & many thanks to Sudeep both for publishing them originally in book form & for his enduring friendship down the years.

Four of my seven books, unusually, and most of the earlier ones (with the exception of *The Lava's Curl*), appeared in bilingual editions : *Gramsci & Caruso* was published with *en face* Czech translations by the late Petr Mikes (& very much at Petr's generous instigation) by Periplum in Olomouc in 2003 & then later in part by Dome Bulfaro & Simona Cesana at Mille Gru in Monza in Italian translation. The two long poems *Mountain Language/Lingua di montagna* & *Journey Across Breath/ Tragitto nel respiro*, with translations into Italian by Cristina Viti, were published by John Rety & Susan Johns at Hearing Eye in London in 2008 & 2011 respectively. They are now republished here without the Italian translations that were, though, totally integral to their first appearance. A third volume in that series has not as yet been completed & thus far remains unpublished. At the same time – with the slight exception of the three 'Arghezi Variations' – we've not included any of my translations in this book, though I have translated widely and deeply. I thank all the above publishers & editors for publishing the poems & for their friendships & support, which is the stuff of poetry.

One of the earliest poem sequences, 'Twenty-Four Hours', dating from the mid-1970s, was transcribed by Rory Cook from the original typed manuscript in 2021 & then published by Prototype & Monitor Books as a chapbook in May 2022, with the lightest of editing.

Eight sections from a much longer (33-section) poem, 'The Conversation With Dante', were included by Seamus Heaney in a special edition of *Ploughshares* that he edited in Spring 1984. I then lost contact with the whole poem, but was fortuitously able to recover these eight sections when I happened upon that edition of *Ploughshares* which had been digitised in the 2000s.

A number of poems written in the late 1970s & 1980s & that weren't included in any of the above books, I've retyped from manuscript with very little or no editing. In general I have not re-written or heavily edited any of these, or indeed any of my poems. Some poems though have been written over a long period of time with lacunae being filled in (or not) after their first version. This is certainly the case with, for instance, two very different poems : 'Stepney Poem' and 'Discourse With The Physicists', both of which were first written in the 1990s & went through various versions before being completed in 2022 & 2016 respectively. In terms of inclusion in the '1975–2005' timespan of this book, I/we have usually been prompted by the date of the first finished version and not the final completion of a poem. I so to speak 'carried' versions, particularly of long poems, around in my head, often for many years before finishing the poems : where a poem first written before 2006 has been finished after then it has generally been included in this volume. A second projected volume will include poems written in or after 2006 and also earlier poems that remain as yet unfinished or unfound or that proved too difficult to edit from variant or part manuscripts in time for this volume.

We'd like to thank Conor Walker for making available to us with such good feeling the newly digitised recordings he'd made for the National Library of Scotland of four readings I gave in Edinburgh in the 1980s (often at the instigation of Tessa Ransford at the Scottish Poetry Library). This alerted us to the text of the poem 'For Sorley MacLean'.

I would also like to thank Arts Council England & their predecessors for generous grant aid in the past (mostly given for my translation work) & also the Royal Literary Fund for recent & current support that has helped me breathe a way through the making of this book : with particular thanks to Kate Griffin & Eileen Gunn respectively.

The unpublished long poem 'Strands, Clusters ...' was written during a six-month residency at the London Hospital in Whitechapel during 2001, when I worked alongside the Community Health Advocates who acted as interpreters in the Hospital, and whose work is utterly vital to people's lives. This poem is dedicated to those extraordinary key workers.

'Mountain Language' & 'Journey Across Breath' were originally written in prose form, as sequences of prose poems which I was never quite satisfied with, before Cristina Viti & I set them out in the 'scroll' form that then felt precisely right for them. Written at some time in the 1990s, they fell into their scroll form (maybe echoing medieval masters) in 2008 & 2011.

'Brick Lane Mela Poem', 'My Mother, Her Tongue' and twelve other poems from *Ancient Sunlight* (Enitharmon, 2014) that were finished or mostly written before 2006 are reprinted as the Birds Of East London section. We would like to thank Enitharmon Press & Stephen Stuart-Smith in particular, both for the original publication & for permission to reprint the poems here.

The 'Siberian Pieces' are from an ongoing, as yet unfinished, gathering of prose poems/pieces, mostly written in the late 1990s & early 2000s. In some I have collaged quotations which are either ascribed in the text, or remain unascribed where I have, for the time being, lost contact with the source.

It's worth saying that I've always written relatively long poems or sequences and that long poems are at the heart of my work. Thus 'Twenty-Four Hours' & 'Praise Poem For North Uist' were among my first finished poems, from the mid-1970s. Other long poems might then be seen to punctuate the whole trajectory of this book, chronologically and in terms of layout : 'Gramsci & Caruso', 'Camões' Voyage To Goa', 'Mountain Language' and 'Journey Across Breath', 'Discourse With The Physicists', 'Strands, Clusters ...', 'Praha Poem', 'Birds Of East London', 'My Mother, Her Tongue', 'Old Women Of My Childhoods', 'Brick Lane Mela Poem' & others. In a sense I feel the whole book is a journey, or trajectory, across breath made by long poems & sequences.

There are too many people to thank, but I want to deeply thank a few : Jess Chandler & Rory Cook for helping me put this book together & Jess for publishing it; Joe Hales for the astonishing proficiency of his layout skills and design; Eleanor Morgan for her support in the early times when many of these poems were written; Tessa Ransford who showed me great support over many years, as also Marius Kociejowski; Hume Cronyn & to continue the Canadian slant, Chris Gutkind; Max Sebald who instinctively drew close to my poetry when many others failed to notice I was a poet; Cristina Viti who has given me her unstinting insight across the years when I was assembling & rescuing this book, as well as translating my work into Italian; Gareth Evans, to whom an extraordinary number of people have reason to be grateful, for all the gist of his support; Sasha Dugdale for her ever-given generosity of praise and insight. And other poet & artist friends who have translated my work into their languages : Adnan al-Sayegh, Golan Haji, Ziba Karbassi, Shamim Azad, Claudiu Komartin, Ana Jelnikar, Hannes Schüpbach & Jèssica Pujol among them. To all these friends & to many others, who I either know, or maybe have forgotten down the dark sepia of time : my wide & grateful thanks !

Stephen Watts, London, August 2022

About Stephen Watts

Stephen Watts was born in 1952. His father was from Stoke-on-Trent and his mother's family from villages high in the Italian & Swiss Alps. He spent very vital time – in place of university – in northern Scotland, especially the island of North Uist, but since 1977 has lived mainly in the richly multilingual communities of the Whitechapel area of East London. Geographies & location (as also their negative theologies) are urgent to his life & his work. Recent books include *Ancient Sunlight* (Enitharmon, 2014; repr. 2020) & *Republic Of Dogs/Republic Of Birds* (Test Centre, 2016; Prototype, 2020) & a b/w 16mm 70-minute experimental film *The Republics* was made from the latter by Huw Wahl in 2019. A book of his 'Drawn Poems' is due from Joe Hales's Sylvia imprint in late 2022. He's also a translator working closely with exiled poets & *inter alia* has co-translated *Pages from the Biography of an Exile* by the Iraqi poet Adnan al-Sayegh (Arc Publications, 2014) & Syrian poet Golan Haji's *A Tree Whose Name I Don't Know* (A Midsummer Night's Press, 2017). A book by the Iranian poet Ziba Karbassi awaits publication & co-translations of two other Iranian writers, Esmail Khoi & Reza Baraheni, are forthcoming from Tenement Press. His translation research was the subject of two recent exhibitions : 'Swirl Of Words/ Swirl Of Worlds' at PEER Gallery, Hoxton, for which he edited a book of that title (its subtitle 'Poems From 94 Languages Spoken Across Hackney' describes it best) & 'Explosion Of Words' with the Swiss artist Hannes Schüpbach, which celebrated his 2,000-page *Bibliography of Modern Poetry in English Translation* at the Straühof Gallery, Zurich, & Nunnery Gallery, Bow, in summer 2021 & 2022 respectively. His own poetry has been translated into many languages, with full collections in Italian, Czech, Arabic, German & Spanish. The present volume gathers together much of his work from the years 1975 to 2005, published & unpublished, & a second volume, including further early & later work, is planned to follow.

( ) ( ) p prototype

poetry / prose / interdisciplinary projects / anthologies

Creating new possibilities in the publishing of fiction and poetry through a flexible, interdisciplinary approach and the production of unique and beautiful books.

Prototype is an independent publisher working across genres and disciplines, committed to discovering and sharing work that exists outside the mainstream.

Each publication is unique in its form and presentation, and the aesthetic of each object is considered critical to its production.

Prototype strives to increase audiences for experimental writing, as the home for writers and artists whose work requires a creative vision not offered by mainstream literary publishers.

In its current, evolving form, Prototype consists of 4 strands of publications:

(type 1 — poetry)
(type 2 — prose)
(type 3 — interdisciplinary projects)
(type 4 — anthologies) including an annual anthology of new work, *PROTOTYPE*.

The tensile resistance in the poems of Stephen Watts, to those intimations of darkness, 'when history was brushing up against the grain', and his empathetic recognition of the subtlest movements of light, is exemplary. And always inspiring. Drawing us outside ourselves. Here is a modest and righteous presence that we are fortunate to encounter on common ground. Walking in a shared city of words, or sending back reports from elsewhere, like generously intimate letters, Watts discovers and discloses his loves and affinities. And there are so many. He is swayed in a kind of rapture, a dance of breath. Shapely patterns open on a meadow of memory, as the poet comes down with the flocks from the mountains. Sequences take flight as the phrases scatter across the page. This collection is a rare gift. It is both a recovery of things that should never have been lost and a path into the dream of a brighter place.

IAIN SINCLAIR

Stephen Watts is a poet constantly aware that he lives in the midst of an abundance of people, places, things, events, asking to be said. A large part of the poetic gift consists in being born into that situation. It is a huge good fortune; but it is also what Rilke called the *Auftrag*, the onus, that which is required of you. The abundance of life, the joy and the grief of it, wants saying. Stephen Watts, lifelong, has been doing just that.

DAVID CONSTANTINE

Openness is too easy a term; Stephen Watts' poems explore it diligently. His, beyond any poetical correctness, is a vast universe where words, birds and humans migrate among the living and the dead; the delight of being alive is offered sharply, yet mercifully the 'I' is no less strange than 'you', no less familiar.

GOLAN HAJI

The work of Stephen Watts is a record of complete sensory experience. These are poems of deep imagery and rhythm, that flex with the details of walks through the lacquered, condensed streets of London; poems that document travels taken on quests of discovery, for the furthering of the art of poetry for all of us. This is what poetry can be: a *movement* before the reader, in which resistance is played out in real time – again and again – each time the poem is enacted. These are poems for the lost voices and the hidden places, for the luminaries of past literatures that Stephen meets as equals in his poems, teasing out the secrets they forgot to tell us. This is work that helps us all to breathe.

CHRIS MCCABE

Stephen Watts' work is protean and yet always strikingly his own. Like Blake, the diction and shape of his poems are made by the sensual experience rather than the organising conventional mind; looking and feeling comes first and only thence the writing, which is an adjunct to being.

SASHA DUGDALE

For Stephen Watts, poetry is 'the blue bag of language': flexible, proletarian, carried everywhere. It's language filled with things. It moves between lives, preserving the trace of breath and body. His London – from Soho Square to Stepney – is woven of the same continuous cloth, even as 'regeneration time' alters its surface. There are good people and bad times; history is fought against and celebrated; and stories are always being passed on through talking, eating, and drinking. Watts' political commitment cuts through *Journeys Across Breath*, showing the work of writing as indistinguishable from that of living. This book provides an extraordinary testament to a life lived in service of people and poems.

WILL HARRIS

What is the point of language, Stephen Watts asks his friends, his readers, a question that ramifies in this exquisite collection. What's the use of speech, if not to talk with you? Stephen's poetry searches – his lines gannet-plunge, island-skim, tower block-ponder, apex-shamble; they are restless and broken, sagacious and kind. No matter the distance nor the perils encountered, Stephen's lines seek the next breath, another answer. In Stephen's poetry, as in life, translation is what makes language possible, variations preserving beauty in the 'harshness of lives'. His poetry fills me with the faith to ask as it teaches me the necessity of quiet – to breathe in the forest, to hear the dead, to hear the songs and silences of everyone who's alive. Quiet, not quietism: Stephen's poetry, his life, acts against the blunt force of monolingualism, against social and environmental dismembering, against the forces that try to un-relate us, to make us forget in the mire of murdered time. Reading Stephen's poetry means meeting people and remembering them fondly, tasting good food, overhearing conversations taking place across space and time, being led to the maelstrom's brink, and guided safely through 'the infinite al-jebr of dreams'. I love this poetry that steeps in so many answers: 'or what is the point of language'.

NISHA RAMAYYA

I am moved and fascinated by Stephen Watts' poetry in ways I find hard to explain and extraordinarily powerful to experience. He is among the most fine and subtle writers I know on the relations of landscape and mind.

ROBERT MACFARLANE

Journeys Across Breath : Poems 1975–2005
by Stephen Watts

Published by Prototype in 2022

Edited by Jess Chandler & Rory Cook
Designed by Joe Hales studio
Typeset in DTL Fell Book
Printed in Great Britain by TJ Books
ISBN 978–1–913513–31–3

( ) (   )   p   prototype

(type 1 – poetry)

www.prototypepublishing.co.uk
@prototypepubs

prototype publishing
71 oriel road
london e9 5sg
uk